T0215033

BUSINESS PLANNING FOR GAMES

This is a practical guide to help budding entrepreneurs think about various planning aspects of their proposed games business, with a view to growing their businesses and becoming more successful. This book includes customary business plan headings and worksheets where the reader can record their thoughts as they start to articulate the vision behind their game.

This is a fresh pedagogical approach to an established method of teaching entrepreneurship that uses a series of worksheets for readers to dip in and out as their needs require. Designed to help nourish an understanding and appetite for doing more than just creating a product, it will help develop an understanding of the business process with sound ideas and inspirational worksheets.

This book will be of great interest to all students learning about the business of games, as well as budding entrepreneurs looking for guidance on how to begin planning their own games business.

BUSINESS PLANNING FOR GAMES

Christopher Buckingham

CRC Press
Taylor & Francis Group
Boca Raton London New York

CRC Press is an imprint of the
Taylor & Francis Group, an **informa** business

Designed cover image: Shutterstock

First edition published 2024
by CRC Press
2385 NW Executive Center Drive, Suite 320, Boca Raton, FL 33431

and by CRC Press
4 Park Square, Milton Park, Abingdon, Oxon, OX14 4RN

CRC Press is an imprint of Taylor & Francis Group, LLC

© 2024 Christopher Buckingham

Library of Congress Cataloging-in-Publication Data
Names: Buckingham, Chris, author.
Title: Business planning for games / Christopher Buckingham.
Description: First edition. | Boca Raton, FL : CRC Press, 2024. | Includes bibliographical references and index.
Identifiers: LCCN 2023027261 (print) | LCCN 2023027262 (ebook) | ISBN 9781032403380 (hardback) | ISBN 9781032403373 (paperback) | ISBN 9781003352594 (ebook) | ISBN 9781032603452 (ebook other)
Subjects: LCSH: Games--Marketing. | Games--Branding. | Business planning. | Entrepreneurship.
Classification: LCC HD9993.G352 B83 2024 (print) | LCC HD9993.G352 (ebook) | DDC 794.068/8--dc23/eng/20230719
LC record available at https://lccn.loc.gov/2023027261
LC ebook record available at https://lccn.loc.gov/2023027262

ISBN: 978-1-032-40338-0 (hbk)
ISBN: 978-1-032-40337-3 (pbk)
ISBN: 978-1-003-35259-4 (ebk)
ISBN: 978-1-032-60345-2 (eBook+)

DOI: 10.1201/9781003352594

Access the Support Material: https://www.routledge.com/9781032403380

Typeset in Caslon
by SPi Technologies India Pvt Ltd (Straive)

Contents

About the Author

Dr Christopher Buckingham is Commercialisation Manager (Social Sciences) at University of Southampton. His priority is to unlock the value and potential of their world-leading social science research outputs and support their translation through commercialisation. He plays a leading role in supporting researchers with identifying potential innovation opportunities, exploring the perceived barriers to commercialising research in the social sciences and the training needs to overcome these barriers. Christopher supports the exploitation of innovations and intellectual property (IP) from the social sciences research base from identification to potential commercial deal-making. Prior to this, he helped create and deliver the undergraduate programme Business of Games and related modules on business for the creative industries. He is an award winning trainer and certified management and business educator.

Acknowledgements

For Harriet, Melita, and Theo.
   Thanks must go to the following for their help and insights:

Adam Proctor
Alex Dunlop
Alison Porter
Annabel Arndt
Ben Clark
David Woolley
Debbie Pinder
Diana Galpin
Eszter Evans for the video productions on level two.
Graham Price
Greg Gibbs
Helen Johnson of UKIE
James Stallwood
Laura Campbell
Lloyd Attrill
Nik Mahon
Ross Popovs
Vanissa Wanick
Will Bateman of CRC Press

No longer with us, but had an influence all the same:

Prof. Ashok Ranchhod (The Guru) – his echoes of wisdom are still often heard.

Crinkle Flatley (AKA Martin Willis) may the Devon dance never end.

Introduction

Business plan writing is a nonlinear pattern of actions that result in a well-researched document that will demonstrate to the reader you have gained some insights into the market, the consumer, and the optimal business model to execute a strategy for success. It sounds neat and tidy with clear expectations that follow in sequence as a reader makes progress through the document and gains clarity on the practice, process, and outcome of the initiative. But this camouflages the real higgidy-piggidy mess that is representative of how most business plans and their strategies get developed. For the business plan document, it is not really about the ability to logically progress from one section to the next but more about the responsibility you have as the author and creator of this plan to determine what gets given a higher weighting in the document and how this can be used to demonstrate the interconnectivity of the various sections.

Readers will be unfamiliar with you and the project you are proposing. They may even be unfamiliar with the sector you write about. Being coherent, cohesive, concise, and consistent means being able to convey the ideas in a way that these people, with potentially no previous experience of the things you talk about, get the gist of the plan you are proposing. This is not to suggest that the way you work should be linear. *Business Planning for Games* is in two levels: level one where we meet the traditional business plan headings and level two where unique worksheets are provided as a way for you to doodle your way through the thinking processes that will lead to insights for your plan.

These are not intended to force you to work from A to B to C and so on. They are there to be used as and when you need them. If you decide to work on the finances and then move to marketing, it is no less valid than one of your peers doing the reverse. *Business Planning for Games* has to be linear; it must be logically ordered to show you the sections and the content that will be needed to make each section as optimal as possible. But that is not meant to reflect the way you must work. You have way more freedom in these decisions. Your working pace and pattern will be your own.

The Caveat?

The output, the final document, should follow the headings in level one. That is the traditional business planning headings should be used to produce the final plan. The document is fixed in time but not inflexible. In the real world, updates are vital to help keep a business plan relevant to the needs and desires of both the stakeholders and the market. But this also brings with it bias. If the plan is being written for investment purposes, care needs to be taken to understand the investors perspective. If you are approaching a traditional finance institution, like a bank, then a conversation with the business relationship manager might add considerable insights into what they expect and what they want to see in the written document. The institution may even have their own templates to use. Likewise venture capitalists (VCs) have their own criteria, getting to know the kinds of areas they invest in, the criteria they use, and the people likely to be scrutinising your business plan will provide you with a stronger case for using their time and money with your project.

Funders are often less interested in your niche game than they are in the overall potential for returns from this project. They have significant costs associated with their activities. The perception of the fat (often male) VCs with dollar signs for eyes is a misplaced image from a time past. Contemporary VCs spend considerable amounts of time appraising the market potential of each project, drawing up legal documentation that covers all parties and keeping abreast of the progress being made. This all comes with a cost and an understanding on the VCs side that many of the projects will fail to cover these costs.

Armed with this knowledge, it becomes more understandable that the strict criteria some of these financial sources use to gauge the potential for the project's seeking funding is a standard that offers a safety net against simply rolling a dice and taking a punt on projects. This is confounded when projects are led by *unknowns*, that is people with strong enthusiasm but no track-record of project success.

We will use the term 'project' in this title to help emphasise the inclusivity of commercial, social, and lifestyle types of organisations that can be developed and brought to market in the games sector.

Structure in Level One

Each section is loaded with questions. Some are more pressing than others.

- These questions appear in the text like this (except for level 2).

This helps them stand out more and makes them easier to find when you go back over a section later.

Structure in Level Two

Level two poses different sets of questions that are unique to each of the boxes found on the worksheets. The worksheets are presented first followed by questions that might help you clarify what exactly you are being asked to do. On some of the questions there are also some hints about where to back-track and find help in Level One. Whereas Level One is intended for external use, Level Two is intended for internal use, and so there are many options on how you complete these work-sheets (for example, doodle, use bullet points, write notes, use images, or brainstorm ideas).

1

EXECUTIVE SUMMARY

There are many reasons for writing a business plan. Knowing the reason why so much of your precious time and energy will be spent on this document is super important. Styles in a business plan change depending on the audience. If the business plan is for internal purposes, then the document will be more relaxed in substance and style. If for external perusal, no matter the purpose, it will be much more professionally written in terms of substance and style. Neither are better or worse, they are simply different and that matters a great deal because for your business you are presenting your personal ideas, values, and insights you have gained about the opportunity. You have enthusiasm, excitement, and a passion for this vision. You want others to feel the same way you do about it. Whether they are already in your team (internal) or you are hoping they might join (external), this is your opportunity to demonstrate to them what is so great about this idea and the time when you have chosen to start it.

1.1 Product and Market Fit

The articulation of the game must be non-technical and clearly stated. Forget about any claims about the digital process of the game, mechanics, dynamics, or aesthetics. These are vitally important to appeal to the players and make the game play the best it can be, but at this stage, in this chapter, we only need to know the essentials of the opportunity that lies at the heart of the project. In simple terms, this section needs to lay out the reason why the game is special and the justification for the claims, all supported by play tests and sound research that prove the creative innovation is needed and desired by a big enough market to make this a viable, feasible, and desirable project to invest resources in.

For game producers, this may present an issue. If the market is small, that means the growth that will be expected by investors is going to be extremely limited. However, it may be the case that you only want to serve a niche market and have very little desire to grow into something bigger. Maintaining a small size and serving this smaller market with your product is fine, but this needs to be clearly articulated from the outset in this section.

Most developers want to explore the possibility of building a sustainable enterprise that can deliver more games in the future. That means they need a decent size market to create returns and reinvest money they make into the business and make it a longer-term project. It must be something that will generate an income for these investors and economically sustain these enterprises.

The market needs to be big enough, have growth, or both (be big and growing). Most of the content that follows in this section will be relevant to those types of enterprises. The games industry is a fascinating mix of different genres of games, all competing for market share, and this makes it important that the intellectual property (IP) you have developed is both original and something people want to buy. Just because you are entering a market that is growing does not, by default, mean you are going to meet sales targets or turn a profit. We will spend more time on this issue later. In this section, you need to convey to the reader the IP that you have created and explain how this IP fits in the marketplace. Part of this is understanding the IP that you have and how you could protect that IP.

This section is not about you but it should be more about meeting a demand that has been created or is out there, a demand that you have witnessed. The focus should be on the innovation in the game. An innovation that will sustain this project over the longer term. In other words, as well as serving a niche in the market and being able to fill that gap you have identified, the innovation needs to use your skills and expertise in the process of generating profit. Everyone sees the world from their own perspective, this makes your view special, and the uniqueness embedded in the innovation needs to be set out in these terms and backed up by the research into the game and the market you have conducted. These areas need to be brought together as you explain the innovation and what led you to this unique insight.

This may have come from seeing how things are done in another place or simply replicating that insight in the context of your own game. It may be that you spotted an opportunity while working on another game, or in a different work environment altogether. This could, for example, result in the use of games to help improve work processes. Or subjective experiences may provide you with an original insight for the innovation at the heart of the game. There need to be clear storytelling elements feeding into this section. So, although it is a serious section, an important function of this section is the overall sketching of the game's development, there is scope for some personal aspects to be included. Your voice needs to be heard because you will be the master of this opportunity.

This helps to demonstrate the uniqueness of the game you have developed and starts to show how the game will stand out in the market. It begins to show how you might promote the business and position yourself in the market against the competition. The real innovation in your game must be the benefits that the customer gains from using or playing your game. This is the only innovation explanation that matters. Everything else is about the features of the game, especially the game proposal document, where the more technical aspects of your game can be outlined. This is not the place for this. This section needs to be as concise and coherent as possible, especially for the non-games specialist as you can make it. The key to success in this section is being able to get the message across about what the game is and how it benefits the customer, the user, and the player. It can help to talk to others who know your game and get their perspectives on what the benefits are. But do not ignore the market, within the context of benefits the market size and the market potential needs conveying in the business plan.

Getting this section right is difficult but rewarding.

1.2 Customers/Users/Players (CUPs)

Whether commercial, social, or a hybrid of these, customers are the lifeblood of any project that seeks to be economically sustainable. In this chapter, it is vital that these people are not only identified but that their desire and need for this product is demonstrated. Right now, this demand is focused on an offer from a competitor. This competitor is already in the marketplace selling their game. This can be problematic as you now must convince these customers to take a different decision and make a purchase from you and what you offer. That demands confidence, especially when your offer is disruptive in the market, something new or radical. If this is the case, then persuading the customers may present an even greater challenge.

- Are you sure they are ready for the new, for the radical?
- Are you sure they are willing to switch and place their trust in you and the game you represent?

If an established competitor exists, the issue is exactly how you will persuade customers to move their allegiance from the existing offer to yours. Your game may be super novel, fresh, and easily understood by these same customers. The game is new, and the market is large and growing. That translates as a potential to find a lot of customers quite quickly who are willing to buy from you. The next question is:

- How often do they buy?

If it's a one-off purchase that is not an issue, but it is a vastly different model to one where the customers continuously return to purchase more products from you. Clarity, as always, is needed.

- Who are these customers?
- Why will customers purchase from you?
- How often will these transactions happen?
- Who are these competitors?

These are all questions that require a coherent, concise, cohesive, and consistent response.

Furthermore, the market you are selling to needs to be big enough for you to be sustainable, it needs to be growing and, in the ideal world, as stated above, the market will be both big and growing. The growth element is concerned with the customers that are available in the market. The main task, therefore, in this section, is to identify who these customers are. The marketing and communications to these people will be explained later in the plan. Here, we need to identify who these people are based on the market research you have conducted. Introducing these as personas for each of the CUPs will add value for the reader of the business plan.

There are many ways to conduct research on your market into who will buy from you. For games, there may also be a further degree of complexity as the CUPs get explained, especially who the users and the players are. This is important because it demonstrates for the reader that you have really understood the market and the different personas in that market that are vital to your game. A good example would be a game for helping piano players practising a tune. The users might be piano teachers as it encourages their students to practise in their own time. But revenues are not from piano teachers. Revenues are generated from the related music products that are advertised in the game.

Therefore, the users are the piano teachers that refer their own students to play the game as stealth learning in their own time. These students are the players. But then the question for the business plan is:

- Who do you target sales activities at?
- Who should you market the game at?

It might help to consider the CUP triangle as shown in Figure 1.1.

The inverted pyramid in Figure 1.1 visually represents the income from a typical CUP configuration. But, of course, this could be mixed up and inverted depending on the game and the income streams generated. Either way, the trick is to identify each of you customers,

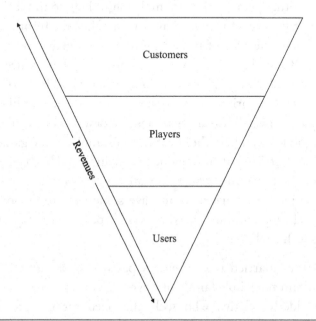

Figure 1.1 CUP revenue triangle

users, and players (CUPs). This is the challenge of doing any research into a market. Until you start trading in the market, there is no real proof that the people you think will buy – will buy from you. As was suggested above, it may also be irrelevant to think of the CUPs as separate personas [hover for explanation 1 PERSONA]. It may be that for your game, the customers are also the players or users. If this is the case, you will still need to conduct thorough research into the personas, but of course this section of the business plan may be lighter as your observations will not need to highlight as many personas.

When we talk about personas, we are talking about your description of these people, a summary of who these people are and things about them that are relevant to the game. You want to show that you have thought about the people that will realistically be the most interested in your game, especially the customers, based on solid research about the market. Research in this context is much wider than people sometimes expect. It tends to look much deeper than simply recording the money these people earn or the websites they get their news from (although, of course, this may well be an element of the research you conduct).

The original concept of persona was used by Carl Jung (1990) to describe the image people project. That is the way that people want, and expect, other people to see them. It might help to think about the persona as the type of person that is your CUP fit. In other words, thinking about the type of person they are and what jobs they do in their lives. If they have jobs to do, then they also have a need to get that job finished. The problem is of course that we all have lots of different jobs to do at various times of the day. Your game is unlikely to be able to help your CUPs do all their jobs in a day. It is better to think of a specific job you can help them with. An example, in the game's context, is for entertainment. Your game may help the CUPs have relaxing and enjoyable down time where they are doing something for leisure. That is the job they must meet to have some time to do something they find relaxing and fun. So, what type of person are they that they need to get this job done?

- A father married to a same sex partner whose turn it is to entertain the whole family one evening.
- An elderly relative who feels the need for inclusion and belonging.

- A geographically dispersed social group that wants to use this leisure time to stay in touch.
- A person that uses this time to build leisurely social networks and support for their real-world self.

There may be hundreds of other reasons for the person wanting this game in their lives. This kind of thinking about the CUPs can at times dramatically shift the thinking about the CUPs as you explore the role the game you have created fits into their lives. But this is just the start.

To get the most out of the 'persona' you need to be able to see the person in the real world. The persona you create for outlining either of the CUPs is a personality created by you as a representation of the type of person you want to serve with this game. There may be more than one type or personality to fit each of the CUP's roles, and that should be embraced. It means you have managed to look beyond simple stereotypes and can see multiple persons with multiple jobs to be completed. All of which can be served via your game. That is a critical point to remember, the game is there to help these people in their lives with specific things they need and desire. Therefore, the research you do, the personas you create and the living pictures this leads to must be as close to the real thing as possible.

But this comes with a caveat. Do not be afraid of being wrong. As we stated earlier in this section, this is guessed work until your game is out there in the real world being played by real people. No one has any real idea how well this game will be received by the market or how well it will serve the intended targets. The ideal is to go beyond satisfying the needs of your CUPs and meeting the desires these people have. This stuff needs to be baked-in to the game. It should be so far embedded within the game that these CUPs do not even think about why they love playing it; it is just there, it is a basic intuition that they should have this game in their lives. Those are big words and 99% of games are not going to get even close to this situation in the real world. But this can serve as an ambition for the game and showing a healthy level of ambition in any executive summary is going to serve the business plan well.

Of course, there are also big dangers in this approach too. Greatly exaggerating the case for the game will have the opposite effect and drive readers in the opposite direction, turning them away from the business plan. Balance is needed. Through balanced levels of assumptions and predictions, based on the facts you have uncovered, via whatever means, will help convince the reader that the authors of the business plan have taken all persona into account and are confident that the jobs these people do will be helped by having this game in their lives.

On the other side is overstating the number of target CUPs that can be met. Not everyone has a job this game will satisfy. Therefore, choosing the personality to focus on in this section is vital. A regular question I get asked is how many CUPs to use. This is an impossible question to answer. Every game is different and the people it serves will also be just as varied. The answer is this; there should be enough detail to provide the reader with confidence that the persona, their job, and their need for the game is accurate and well presented. It might also be worth noting at this point that the purpose of the game (see Section 1.3) is aligned well with the CUP personas presented. Again, this is confidence building for the reader, it is showing the reader that this game can make a difference for the people being targeted, and that the game is a good match with their needs and desires. Beyond this, the customers will have sufficient awareness of this game and the value it creates for them that they will buy into this vision.

The real issue is 'their' needs and desires as opposed to 'your' needs and desires in creating the game. That may seem a bit obvious, but I have seen this in so many business plans. The order in these circumstances is that the game gets made and then an audience is sought. Imagine for a moment if this was in the reverse, imagine that you have an audience identified that you want to serve and you make the game based on these inputs. This brings us full circle to the concept of baking-in the need for the game. How beneficial would that be, to have this present right at the start of the design stages for the game. It would mean an even better fit between your game and the CUPs.

These approaches are about listening to the needs of the CUPs. Let us call these approaches; 'game first' and 'market first' where the 'game first' approach follows methodologies that place the game designer as the focus. They decide on the game dynamics and mechanics based on their own perceptions of the CUPs needs and desires. In other words, game design in this approach is based on their paradigm of the market [hover for explanation 02 PARADIGM].

The 'market first' approach is the opposite. Here the game designer listens to the market's desires, needs, and then sets about attempting to satisfy these desires and needs with their game. This means data collection, analysis, and interpretation by the game designer (and/or their team). This sounds more objective than the 'game first' approach, but this is not necessarily the case. Avoiding bias in the interpretation of the results from any research is always an awkward thing to achieve. But this latter approach can mean the use of more quantitative methodologies being employed.

Most game designers and their studios use a mix of these approaches to studying their games. Designers and game makers are more likely to think about the game mechanics, dynamics, and aesthetics (MDA) (Hunicke et al., 2004) before they really consider the CUPs in an economic sense. The emphasis is very much on the player. Game designers have a particular paradigm, and this leads them to make games. That is not a criticism, some of these games have been successful. But for the games that do not have pure entertainment at the heart of the game, games that serve another, higher (?) purpose, but being a little more on the 'market first' approach might help develop games that are a better fit with their intended audiences (Buckingham & Wanick, 2021). This is within the context of entrepreneurship and the associated risks; the business plan needs to show the reader that the risks are as low as possible. This means the research conducted must be written in such a way that the reader can easily see what was done, the analysis that was conducted, and the results that have been extrapolated from this enquiry. The game should always be built around these insights.

1.3 Aims + Objectives

This section provides the business plan reader with a briefing of what the overall outcome of any activity in the project will result in. More details can be added in Section 2.2, when we move to the paradigm for the project. Here the concern is with the type of enterprise you are going to build and what the overall aims and objectives of the project are. In other words, what you want to accomplish and when you want to realise these achievements. At this point these should be limited and controlled. They need to be realistic, and they need to be achievable by you and your team or the people supplying you with the things you need to make this game. For many past students of mine, this bit sounds the easiest and it is often not until they start to drill into what is needed and what the results of all this activity will be that they begin to see how complex writing the business plan can be.

But first, let us set out exactly what we mean by aims and objectives. An aim, in this context, is a smaller step that will be taken to achieve a longer-term, overall objective. An objective, in this context, can be thought of as a combination of steps (aims) that you have taken along your project's journey. An important thing to remember is that not all these steps need to be taken by you alone. Many can be tasked to others who are more capable than yourself to achieve specific things. This is a crucial point; many entrepreneurs when they start out can forget that help is available, and it may not cost as much as they think. Marketing is a classic example. Some of the most creative and effective marketing activities have cost almost nothing to create and can have a lasting impact.

Quite often marketing can be seen as this void in which money gets poured with no real sense of what value it adds to the project. Firstly, that really is an unhelpful way to think about marketing. Secondly, why spend money on a game you have no idea is going to be as valued as you are predicting? A better option is to think about a strategy that will cost very little in financial terms and lead to buzz being created around your game. Could you do a mob-play in your local park, join a tech jam, help a charity, or aid local people with a specific learning issue? All could be helpful to others and get you some much needed media coverage. All these things can be done with little financial output while generating significantly more interest in your game. Which option you choose, and this list is by no means exhaustive, depends on what you are trying to achieve.

- What are your aims and objectives?

A prerequisite therefore is that you complete the vision and mission statements in Chapter 3. That is because any decision you take concerning the aims and objectives will be based on your own values (see Section 2.2) and the way you see the world from your own set of interests and concerns. This may sound a bit 'new age' for a section on aims and objectives but remember things must be linked and they do not have to cost a lot of financial resources to implement. The people you meet along the entrepreneurial journey may well be in position to help you think about these areas. According to Fisk (2008), there are seven life stages of an entrepreneurial project; create, launch, stabilise, extend, mature, evolve, and exit. This is a massive generalisation about the stages a firm goes through. But they may be useful when trying to think through what the overall objectives are for the longer-term situation of the project.

For some users of this book, the creation stage has been given the greatest attention and an idea for a game has already emerged (or at least started to form). Alongside the refinements being made to this idea of a game, you should also be thinking ahead to the launch stage. How will you get the game out there and in the hands of your customers, while also thinking through how you capture their responses to the game?

That is a 'now' problem and to make firm statements on how this will be achieved means you also need to know something of the timelines you are planning to work on. It might help to think back to 'then', to reflect on how you have got to where you are to date. The reflection is important as it connects your culture to the aims and objectives you want to accomplish. It hints for the reader what kind of culture they are dealing with (this will be developed in Chapter 3). The importance the reader will place on this aspect will be determined by their motivation for reading it in the first place. This aspect may be important to them.

Thinking this way forces us to neglect for a moment the most important reason for writing a business plan in the first place, the solidifying of your ideas and the opportunity to express these in a codified document. Think about it for a moment. How many times in your life will you be able to be selfish enough to write about something you are passionate about?

For most of us, the answer is not often enough. For many of us the same is true about the culture we are going to develop in our project. Understanding the culture can really help define who and what your project is about. It is not complicated; it is about the routines of your project and the interactions these produce among your people.

Whether they are employed by the project or freelancers that come in and serve the project's needs when required. The expectations and the standards are the things that feed into your culture. It can concern working patterns, dress codes, or more symbolic things like who gets to sit where in the office. These things all matter because they serve to define the character of the project and can help to make it a more appealing place for people to come and work at. This can have a multiplying effect as others want to join this funky environment, they want to be part of it. The appeal now spreads. In terms of the aims and objectives, this needs to be stated as more than just a nice element of what is planned. There must be genuine signs that the culture will be strong by explaining, in brief, the things that are valued and the things that will be done to achieve these. In other words, it is not just about words, it must also be about actionable criteria that help create and then reinforce this culture [hover for explanation 03 CULTURE].

It may seem obvious to some, but this brings us to Chapter 2 (vision) and Chapter 3 (mission). This is the 'next' part where the culture needs considering in terms of how this will tie in with the vision and mission. These tell the world the purpose of the project. Beyond this, culture also needs to take account of the values that have been identified as important for you as the founder of the project. These are your opportunities to demonstrate diversity and inclusion in the culture of the project. The danger is that these act as nice ways to help sell the idea of the project to others. To be meaningful, these need to be real and things that are out there and acknowledged by the people in the team as and when they join.

A good example of this was with a start-up that provided free pizza one afternoon per month. Alongside the pizza were discussion tasks that were focused on the culture. This provided the founders with some real insights into how people felt working on the project and some ideas about what was working, what was not working and, more importantly, what might be done to help make things even better. It was a simple and fun approach which helped founders reflect on the approaches they had adopted. With this they better understood the identity of the project, and this helped to feed their marketing activities. There were issues with the idea, but it was at least an attempt to use a more dynamic approach to learning about the culture they had helped create. Plus, who does not love free pizza?

There were risks with the approach outlined above and this idea is not replicable to every project. But risk is a major concern when addressing the aims and objectives of the project; these risks, and the rewards, need quantifying (more will be explored on this in Section 4.4). Risk is always present in any project that seeks to engage customers, users, or players. Clarity is needed when the plan outlines the tolerance of the founders towards risk. These risks should be stated as minimal, because with sound planning and research, these will be balanced and thought through by the team at a much deeper level. But when creating the overall strategic aims and objectives, risks should not be ignored. They can be very real and have a detrimental effect on the ability of the project to survive. Equally though, some projects are minimal in terms of their ambitions, and this will reflect lower levels of risk exposure. For example, if all you want to do is create games, then being able to meet your monthly survival budget (see Chapter 8) might be enough to enable you to do this. You will not need to be writing a business plan as this will be a hobby project and not an ongoing entrepreneurial project. But contrast that with someone looking to build a sustainable business with the explicit intention of selling it within five years. Or with a different person seeking to build a games studio that will be sustainable over the next 10 to 15 years, capable of not just surviving future iterations of technology, work patterns, social norms, and cultural demands in their games, but a studio that thrives as it does so, because it has flex built in.

The risks involved in the above scenarios are vastly different, but so too are the rewards. These rewards can be expressed as financial or as some other benefit for the energy that will get consumed in developing the project. These aims and objectives will be impacted by the culture.

- What does your brand, and this game, stand for?
- How does that translate into what you want to do and achieve?

These can be tough questions, but they need answering to serve the business plan and the reader. It adds clarity for them in that they can determine where they think you are heading and where you want to be at some future point in time. But this is also true for internal motivations for writing the business plan. It helps you, the project lead, and the team get a better sense of where this thing is going and the overall direction of travel. But of course, your aims and objectives must be based on solid research that provides you with confident and sound insights on what is possible and likely.

1.4 Values

Having established the 'special sauce' in the game (see Section 1.1), you can now start to consider your own values and the goals that you wish to achieve. The key here is to make sure that these goals are aligned with your personal values. That means that the commercial goals embedded within the strategy for the game, and the business venture, need to match in some way and allow you to achieve the goals while not impinging on your values. In short, you need to be able to sleep at night while creating this project.

Values change dramatically from person to person, and this makes it important to recognise that there are no set right and wrong answers in this chapter. However, it is an opportunity for you to demonstrate how your values, as stated in Section 2.2, are matched with the goals of the project. Think through these goals and make a list, this then feeds this section as we start to outline what these are and indicate for the reader how they align with the project holistically.

Let us imagine for a moment that the values you most want to focus on in the project are the enhancement of others by teaching them about 'X' (goal). The game could be a serious game with educational outcomes that will help players recognise 'X' and understand how this affects their behaviour.

A further goal of the business is to survive and thrive; you want it to be a sustainable enterprise that will develop and deliver games that are worthy because they create value for others through instruction and education on issues that are hard to discuss in other contexts. A good example of these kinds of issues is 'X'. The business, therefore, will develop games in the niche area of serious games that are initially focused on 'X'. In the longer term, issues such as 'Y' and 'Z' may also form the basis for future games. Although a niche, this market is huge with sufficient customers to make the business economically sustainable.

In the above example, you can see how the specific desire of the project's creator (you) is well aligned with the goals of the project (create and sustain an economically viable game business). It is not complicated, and it is not overly ambitious in any of the claims that it is making – in fact, it clearly articulates that some thought and research has been done on the size of the niche.

Even though exact figures are not provided, we get a sense that the author is confident that their appraisal of the situation is a good one. As a reader, we start to feel confident about this. It makes sense and even though we have no idea what 'X', 'Y', and 'Z' represent; we can get a sense of the kind of thing that the project wants to achieve in the longer term.

Of course, values are also able to focus more on the development of an individual or on the use of technology to help support the project in the future. But this becomes a little more difficult as we do not know what technology will be developed in the future or how useful it might be to our project and game. For example, quantum computing could be fantastic bits of kit in the future, but we have no real idea how it will disrupt the status quo of any sector. For example, could it:

- Replace social media?
- Make gaming even more social?
- Replace platforms that host these games?
- Revolutionise streaming?

We have no idea, but the dynamic capability to have your finger on the pulse of what is happening in your games sector will help demonstrate to the reader that you are, at the very least, considering and reflecting on this stuff and making some form of contingency plan that may herald disruption in your market(s) and even to the special sauce in your game. It must be remembered that the social context of this dynamism is also vital. People are the CUPs; they are at the heart of what you do.

Markets are always in flux, and so is the social context of these markets. If we are looking to tell a reader about how our values and goals are aligned, then we cannot dismiss the background stuff that is happening in the environments we operate in. We will be looking at the STEEPLE and SWOT analysis tools in Chapter 5. These simple tools help us to recognise some of the background context in which we operate daily. This is important to consider as this can have a serious impact on the critical issues we address in the games we develop and the wider business context in which we operate.

More importantly for this section of the plan, the background context of the social aspects may even impact our game. This can have various consequences for what we are trying to achieve and the goals we have set for the project. We can think of this section as setting our evidence and proof that we get the context in which we operate. We could explain, for example:

- Explain the sector and how we see the sector operates now and in the future.
- The competition that exists and how they are aligned with their markets.
- Shifts and trends that you see emerging in the next few years.
- STEEPLE changes that have the potential to impact the project more directly.
- A justification for the time frames when we discuss any of the above factors.

We can conceptualise the goals we need to consider as being split between being planned for and needing action in some form. The important thing in this model (Figure 1.2) is that we do not lose sight of the left-hand side (mission and vision statements and purpose), which serves to help the planning process and indeed start to outline the things we need to consider when getting the planning process started. The right-hand section (chores and actions) denoted the things we need to do; these are in some ways more tangible and demand more immediate action than the left-hand side of the model. These two sides serve a different function to one another. There are unique needs between the mission and vision statements, the purpose, the chores, and the actions. But they should not be seen separate as they directly intersect with one another. Most importantly, they are there to serve the project. Bear that in mind when you start writing this section and you should be able to produce something that lends

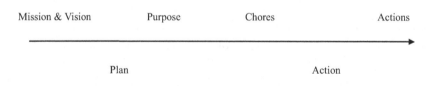

Figure 1.2 The Pyramid of Goals. (Barrow et al., 2008: 32).

itself well for a reader to comprehend the nature of the project and what exactly the goals and values are that have led the project so far and will continue to drive the project in the future.

On the planning side, you can use the mission, vision, and purpose to think through the strategy that will help deliver on the aims and objectives of the overriding plan. On the action side, the chores are first; these are the list of things that will need doing. They are a list of pointers for achieving the plans on the left-hand side. We call them chores as these are things that need to be done. You may like doing them, but they are necessary for achieving the plan. We end with the actions that will be taken to make the plan a reality. These are the chores made into a definitive set of things that will be done. Note to the linear nature of the model. We move from conceptual understanding to an actionable outcome. This is super important because the best plans are nothing without some action to make them a reality.

References

Buckingham, C. & Wanick, V. (2021), Crowdfunding Serious Games: Towards a framework. In Fabio Perez Marzullo & Felipe Antonio de Oliveira (eds), *Practical Perspectives on Educational Theory and Game Development*, Hershey, PA: IGI Global.

Fisk, P. (2008), *Business Genius*, Chichester: Capstone.

Hunicke, R., LeBlanc, M., & Zubeck, R. (2004), MDA: A formal approach to game design and game research, In *AAAI Workshop on Challenges in Game AI* (Vol. 4).

Jung, C.G. (2021), III The Persona As A Segment Of The Collective Psyche, In Violet S. de Laszlo (ed), *The Basic Writings of CG Jung*, pp. 140–146, Princeton University Press.

2
VISION

This chapter is the most grandiose of all sections in your business plan. At least that should be the case. The term vision is itself dated and this section could be called *optimism* instead. For some that may capture the real benefits of this section. It shows any reader, internal or external, how the world is going to be with this game in it. How the world will benefit from the very existence of the game and how humanity will be changed forever. Sound too much?

That is the point. A vision statement should be wild and expensive. Never use the first attempt at this bit of writing the business plan as there will be several versions written out before you finally get to the version that is both coherent and cohesive enough that you feel ready to share that vision with the world. Because it must be shared at some point. Readers need to get a feel for the passion that you have for this game, the vision statement should be short and to the point. It needs to convey the essence of what will be achieved by the game. This should be focused and needs to show what will be in place once the game inhabits a market.

It must also quantify something about the expectations of the project in terms of market share, number of CUP's, financial revenues, and returns, and how things will be transformed once the game is out there in the world. There should be some clarity added to this point.

We know this vision thing sounds to some a lot like the mission and the strategy for the project. But these are quite different things that serve very distinct purposes. Chapter 3 will deal with the mission in more depth. But the mission is where you set out the actual things the project will do in terms of the CUP's that will be served and the overall purpose of the project. It might help to think of the vision as an idealistic future where the world is a better place because of this project's existence. The mission, on the other hand, is more grounded and describes the reality of what the project does, and for

DOI: 10.1201/9781003352594-2

whom. Both these have elements of strategy (see Section 3.1) in them. Strategy, according to Rumelt (2011: 54), is about acting, to quote Rumelt; 'The purpose of good strategy is to offer a potentially achievable way of surmounting a key challenge.

This can be summarised in both the mission and strategy as being about action and doing things, while vision is more about ambition, predicting a future where the project is more than needed, and is desired by both CUPs and you. That is a good place to start:

- What makes people want to play this game?
- What makes this game super attractive and draws CUPs in so that they want to consume the game?

Answer these questions coherently and you have a good set of responses to help feed the vision statement. The issue for many in the creative sector is not the use of imagination to think about these future scenarios, nor is it an issue of being creative in the approach to writing a narrative. The issue is more often about 'your' game. Being able to see and convey the real value that you want people to experience in your game. The danger is that you start to think about how the game works, what makes the images stand out or the sound help tell a narrative or the intersection of the die with the board or any number of interactions that combine to create the game itself. This stuff is needed but not in these representations. These are the features of your game; what we are seeking in this section is the wholesome benefits of the game for the world. Quantify these, and you should start to see a better vision statement emerge. But this brings us full circle, back to the place where you need to articulate the vision for the game. So let us see some examples of how you could write this out. But before we do, it is essential to remember that this is an iterative process, which means this is not a once and done exercise. It means it is ongoing and needs reflection to get the balance right for the business plan. Returning to it frequently is the key to writing a good one. So, let's look at one:

We are going to look at the Japanese corporation, Konami. They offer the investor a particularly granular view of the four segments they operate in. They call these 'businesses', and they consist of *digital entertainment business, amusement business, gaming and systems business*, and *sports business*. In turn, these are all held by one umbrella company, Konami Group Corporation. In business parlour, this is called a 'holding' company. The holding companies' vision is the most interesting, it states:

> By responding sensitively to the latest trends and consistently taking on new challenges, Konami Group has been an endless source of creativity and innovation since its establishment in 1969. In the business areas of "entertainment" and "sports", we have provided customers with a diverse range of products and services through four segments: the Digital Entertainment Business, the Amusement Business, the Gaming & Systems Business, and the Sports Business. Through continuing its legacy of tirelessly taking on challenges, the Konami Group will realize new possibilities by expanding our reach over an even wider area to provide people around the globe with dreams and everyday excitement.
>
> *(Konami Group Corporation, 2022)*

Konami has a long history of serving their customers. They are a well-established player in their field and are listed on both the Tokyo and London stock exchanges. But looking at the statement above, we can get a sense that they are not resting on their legacy products, they are seeking new opportunities and new ways to expand and serve their customer segments. The goal is, of course, to make dreams a reality for people all over the world. In fact, not just a reality, but an *exciting* reality.

What this means in reality is open to interpretation by most external observers reading this statement. On the same page they state their aim as:

> We, the Konami Group, aim to be an enterprise that will continue to keep our stakeholders always looking forward with anticipation as we create and provide our current and future customers with products and services that offer "Valuable Time".
>
> *(Konami Group Corporation, 2022)*

This corporation are very good at doing what they do, but the point is some content in your vision statement will be objective, easily understood, and quantifiable, while some content will be more subjective and more difficult to express. These are also more likely to be the things that readers feel less confident about. Reflection must play a role in the creation of the vision statement and the expression of what the world will look like with your game in it. There may be subjective areas of the strategy that need to be expressed as a quantity in your vision (and in your mission). Be ready to consider these areas if they are a principal element of the vision for the future. What you are showing to the reader is that you have considered these areas and understand the implications for the game. Konami is a massive organisation; they can afford to be opaque about their actual intentions and what the terminology in their corporate statements mean. But you don't have this luxury. As a small game developer, you have to be more explicit because the type of reader for your statements in your business plan are going to need to be able to get the gist quickly and make sense of your intentions.

Beyond this, it also helps develop a sense of confidence for the reader. The reader views the author as an effective strategist that is taking decisive action to locate and measure the elements they talk about in their vision. Crucially, these elements are based on facts you have uncovered. But as with any element of predicting future states of being, there is of course always a danger that stated assumptions are misguided or wrong. Another reason they should always be based on the data you have managed to uncover is to allow for more accuracy with the predictions you make. Predictions must be understood in the context of the game and used to guide decisions being taken in the present. Therefore, the things that readers will want to know when reading your vision statement is that the market can sustain the project and that the true advantages and strengths of the project are accurately being portrayed. Konami do not have the same need to justify these things.

This leads us away from the vision statement and forces us to consider the reality of the paradigm we are expressing now this project is in the world. The project, as we will see, is fixed in the pages of the business plan. What gets presented there is a solid portrait of the project and how it will be implemented. A superb understanding of the market and even greater confidence around who the CUPs are and why they will take purchasing decisions in your favour. But reality could not be further from these truths. That is because to be truly effective a vision needs to be able to flex and wane as new data and interpretations of reality are added to the project mix. This means all team members need to have their fingers on the sector's pulse, be able to listen, digest current information, and make confident decisions based on this fresh input. The key here is an ability to learn and be decisive about what this learning means for the project.

2.1 Sector

Asking which sector you operate in is often taken for granted. It is at times considered so obvious that it does not need addressing. To some the answer seems obvious, you are in the games sector. But even though this may be true, this is a massive sector, so which bit have you decided to serve?

This is the main fundamental question that needs addressing. Games are products of various forms, card, board, dice, or video and so on. Furthermore, are these social, solo, first person, epic, or educational? Knowing this is the starting point to finding out who you serve and thinking about how a well-played game (de Koven, 2013) might be made for this sector. Know this and you start to understand the sector. It also means that the simplicity of the first questions asked above can be answered with confidence. There is complexity in the question that helps us understand the product and the value for our CUPs.

It is that value that really counts here. Because unless we know and understand that value, we do not really know or understand the motives for the CUPs. If, on the other hand, we spend a little time thinking about this, we can start to think about the benefits we create for these CUPs. By knowing the benefits, we produce for the CUPs, we can better communicate with these people. Think about that for a moment. The game may remain the same, but the design means that the game produces different experiences for different CUPs. The CUPs' experiences are different because the rules of their engagement with the game, the reason they are a customer, a user or a player is the thing they seek, and it is the value they want in their lives. Know this and you can craft messages that demonstrate this attainment for each of them. The game does not change. The mechanics, dynamics, and aesthetics remain. But the value can change and therefore the message must also be relevant and emphasise that value.

As an example, think again about the piano teacher we met earlier. Let us call them Padma. Padma's needs are different from their students. Padma needs a tool that can complement their lessons for their learners. Let us imagine the learners are mostly children, under the age of 16. So, Padma's customers are the guardians and parents of these children. They pay him for the service he provides. Any advertising Padma does to the parents will need to show how wonderful their children's futures will be because they have learned to play the piano with Padma. Not with a competitor, but with Padma.

If on the other hand Padma decides to teach a wider target group, let us say retired people who have always wanted to learn, but never had the time until now. The message Padma uses to attract these people needs to be different to the one used for the parents/guardians of the children. This is one of the advantages of thinking through which sector you are in. The sector is less important than the CUPs in that sector. But it means potential for a more tailored and focused message being broadcast to potential CUPs. The product remains the same (piano lessons), but the message gets changed as different CUPs are communicated with. Like anyone, these CUPs also want to know the benefits they receive, not the features of the product.

This means our piano teachers need to think accurately about what these benefits are and then incorporate that understanding into their messages. For example, their customers are parents. Parents might want to benefit their children by giving them discipline that makes them more confident in life. The feature of the lessons can provide this by regular, highly structured lessons that have a clear path and progression. Most people with children will tell you that these features of progress are not how they will persuade their children to take-up the lessons. The message here is more likely to be something like *Hey kids, want to be more Elton John? Learn piano.* You can see how the features and the benefits are quite different in terms of the wording used. The product is the same, (piano lessons), but the message is quite different.

Bringing this back to games, let us imagine you have developed a game for mobile devices that really helps students learn to play the piano. The game is serious, but fun to play.

- What sector are you in?
- Are you in the mobile development sector?
- The music sectors?
- The serious games sector?

You may even consider your game to be in all these sectors, a spread across different purposes. But even if you were right about that,

- How would the message change in each of the sectors identified?

To answer that you need to think about the target market you are aiming at and the benefits these people will gain. Think about the essentials of what these people gain from your game. You should know this as it should have informed your core game mechanics (Salen & Zimmerman, 2004). Use this knowledge to help you think about the benefits. For example, PAC-MAN (Bandai Namco Entertainment, 1980) uses a joystick to move the yellow disc and avoid the ghosts. A benefit could be hand and eye coordination, a benefit to everyone as they grow up, especially if the player is going to be a future pianist, surgeon, or fighter pilot. Either way, she will need good coordination which could be helped by playing Pacman.

A simple table might help to demonstrate how this might work:

Row one in Table 2.1 is the core mechanics. The easiest element to understand for game designers. But it is tempting to replicate the same detail across all CUPs. It might be accurate to do so, but equally there might be additional stuff that gets added to shift the core mechanics for specific groups. For example, a core mechanic for the player might not be understood by the customer. Although it remains the same core mechanic, the way this gets communicated might be different. There may also be core mechanics that change depending on the ability of the user. In this case, the core mechanic(s) may be adjusted to accommodate the specific needs of each group. It follows therefore that this personalisation of the game's mechanic, to meet the physical or mental ability of the groups identified, will require additional levels of communication. The benefits have shifted, only a little, and this needs to be conveyed because these personas are CUPs in this sector.

Table 2.1 CUPs Features versus Benefits

	I CUSTOMERS	II USERS	III PLAYERS
1 Core Mechanics	1i	1ii	1iii
2 Features	2i	2ii	2iii
3 Benefits	3i	3ii	3iii

Doing so brings more than just a commercial benefit for the project, it also helps feed the cognition of the reader. Even so, for a vast majority of games, the core mechanics will remain the same for each persona in the CUP categories. There may be other dimensions that also need adding, changes to these mechanics, that result in greater diversity and inclusion in the CUPs for the game. If this is the case, be explicit about the celebration of this dimension.

Row two are features. For customers, these need to be focused on what the game provides them. In our example, the piano game's features are the logical progression that can be realised by the player. The customer is paying for these very features. So how do we translate these into a language that makes sense to them and adds value for them?

2i Customer: Imagine advertising being shown for piano-related goods. Advertisers and creative agencies are our customers.

2ii User: For the teachers, these features might be the ability to coordinate the game with the specific lesson they have been delivering.

2iii Players: Specific scales with time to practise, away from the lessons as homework. For example, practising the techniques and scales that they learn as they move through the weekly lessons means they get to be better piano players.

Row three are benefits. These are the essential things to communicate because these are the motivators for the CUPs in our example. Therefore, it is essential to get this right and to be able to signal to the CUPs what these are on their terms so they can understand what the benefits to them are.

3i Customer: Small price for a wide coverage of targeted segments.

3ii User: They get to enhance their offer and make their lessons more relevant.

3iii Players: Simply improve with regular use of the game. They get to be better piano players.

Row three can be used to communicate with the diverse groups which makes the communications much more appropriate for the segment being targeted (see Section 5.2). More important is your own understanding of the market you serve. If you need to compose a business plan, then you may need to convince others how well-thought-out the whole project is. Making the case for understanding the sector or convincing others that you belong in one sector as opposed to another can help build confidence in the plan for the readers and help them to understand the case for the project. In other words, it can add clarity for any reader of the plan, whether as internal or external members of the project. This is the greatest benefit of this section.

2.2 Value versus Values

As developers of games, in all their wonderful mixes, and more than most other industries, we are hypersensitive to the needs of our players. There are times when I have been so focused on the development of the game and the experience for the player that I have forgotten about the wider sociocultural context of what I am doing and more than that, why I am doing it.

Having a clear set of key values serve a distinct purpose of telling the reader what the project is trying to do for its customer base. These customers can be multiple, in which case each one will need explaining with clear quantifiable outcomes. Normally, this is expressed as sales or as profits against the trading costs of the enterprise (see Chapter 8), but not always. When we say these need to be quantifiable, we mean measured. To be effective and to persuade a reader of the need for the value being delivered in the game, it needs concrete research to support the ideas being put forward. This may be from the end user (player) or the person who purchases the game (the customer).

This translates into a market that is happy and willing to engage with the game and/or make a purchase. This latter scenario is of course an economic outcome of the interaction between the buyer and the game. The key value in the project may go beyond economic transactions. A game's goals may be to seek more diverse audiences or gain peer recognition, and these may be key value metrics to be measured. It should be remembered that it does not necessarily directly produce any income or revenue for the project, but it may add to the overall value of the project in the minds of the target demographic. That is important as it has the potential to lead to business growth and build a positive reputation for the game in the longer term.

Another perception may be produced in the mind of the user/purchaser when the game develops concepts of quality or fairness that can lead to better connections with the customers you wish to attract. Revenues are not a priority at this stage, rather the focus is on the creation of *value* for the customer. This has a cost that must be recouped later in the economic transactions that take place, but the priority, before sales are realised, is to create the tangible and intangible value that will aid the connection with the target and facilitate behaviour that will lead to sales. The value is the trigger for this behaviour; so, it is the trigger that we need to focus on here in this section. That trigger needs to be logical and clearly articulated for the reader. It will involve branding, marketing, and the perceptions internally of the game developer and externally of the end user and the purchaser. As in all projects, whether commercial, social, or a hybrid, dangers lie in these being misaligned.

The value that gets created must create a symbolic connection with the target demographic. This happens through the interactions and the perceptions of the game that the branding and marketing produce. This can lead to better perceptions of the game as something that will add value for the target. There are people that take offence at the concept of the term 'target' being used to describe the people the project wants to attract. Some prefer the term 'objective' as in *the objective of the exercise is to attract a certain customer base*. But we shall use target as this is a more appropriate term that can be applied to the end user (player) or the person that makes the purchasing decision (customer). The point is that the communication that happens in the market with the targets needs to produce the right perceptions in that target's mind.

Communication therefore serves to build better and stronger connections with the targets and then where possible reinforces these connections with ongoing conversations. Therefore, this section needs special attention and careful consideration in order that the purpose of the enterprise is clearly defined and a strategy for the communication of the value makes sense given the overall mission and vision. In this case, the way the world looks at the project, the paradigm should be embedded in the mission and vision. The values in this paradigm must be specific and aligned with the overall objectives of the project. When trying to convey these to the reader, there is a danger that the novice game developer will try to include too many values to be measured in the plan. It is far better to select two or three that are most likely to produce an outcome you recognise as being a success, and to think about how this will be translated into something that can be measured.

There may be multiple targets for the game. In this case, each one will need to be outlined in the plan and given a justification for their inclusion. However, the value that each target gains from the game must be clearly articulated and backed up with real-world findings. Each category needs to be restrained in the value that gets produced and measured for each of the target groups selected. Otherwise, the project will appear stretched and over optimistic in the approach being adopted. This is more common than you might expect, especially with inexperienced authors of these kinds of plans.

Another aspect of this section is how well you understand your personal drivers. The things that get you up in the morning, the things that you know you will be doing, and so give you an additional bounce in your step as you raise yourself up and make that first tea for the day. These passions and drives are the stuff of values; they add value for you by being the things that motivate you to step forward with energy. They stoke your fire and provide you motives and put a smile on your face at the thought of doing these activities.

This is the difference between value and values. Where value adds something for you and others, your values tend to act as a guide, enlightening the path towards the value you seek. Principles, moral codes, and ethical perceptions are all elements of the values mix that make-up you. Their guidance is often implicit during the action (and choices) you make. Action that leads to values, in some form, being created. For most entrepreneurs', values are not something we sit down and attempt to map out or articulate in some form. But by doing so, we can better grasp the real motivation we have for the lives we have shaped and the decisions we make.

Values also tend to be fixed. They tend to be embedded within our character, part of the baggage we carry around with us. Values are often influenced by the social conditions we were exposed to as children. We learn these values and they in turn help us be ourselves. They help us work out our identity and even grant us enthusiasm by helping us realise the things we find joy in.

From an entrepreneurial perspective, this needs considering so as the ethical position of the project can be balanced with you. At the end of the day, you have constructed the project, and so the project should reflect those things you consider important. This can be on a very wide spectrum that can be focused on almost any aspect of life. Having as small an impact on the environment as possible, supporting literacy in a world state, helping victims of crime, or making modern slavery more visible are all examples where values play an element in the project's existence.

In the United Kingdom, NESTA emphasises the importance of this aspect for either commercial or socially driven projects. They produced a booklet in 2011 which among other things had a section dedicated to values. They even went as far as to produce a list of values that one could choose from as the user mapped out the things they considered important. Things that made up the reader's values. This was inauthentic; it was an exercise in making the reader confront a unique and overlooked aspect of the justification for them to start a project in the first place. But it was also an immensely powerful exercise as it asked readers to confront and reflect on the things that dwell inside. Positives and negatives were laid bare for the reader to reflect on at some future stage. I can still remember my thoughts when our facilitator at the NESTA workshop I was attending, Percy, explained what we were going to do. My reaction was to label the exercise as hippy claptrap that would have no other purpose than to make NESTA look good when feedback was requested at the end of Percy's session. But I was wrong.

The exercise was so powerful it has stayed with me and has influenced some of the work I have done. It helped me see the real guiding principles for any of the ventures I subsequently got involved with. The important thing was that it was not about the money. It was about service to others. Money is super important; I am not trying to pretend I am some sort of anti-capitalist hero. Far from it. But it did open my eyes to the idea that whatever I do, wherever I decide to hang around for a while, it must sit well with me. I must sleep at night. My sleep has helped knowing I have added value for others. My core values are constructed in such a way that I crave adding value for others.

For each of us, it will be something completely different. The difference does not really matter; these are our values. They are personal, some may be shared with others, and some may be personal. To give a simple example; if you and I were doing some business in a state where bribes were part of the culture, we may be equally offended and appalled at the idea. Me less than you, but the degree of repulsion felt is significant, the fact that we both have a value reference that means we are on the same page. We are equally against bribes being paid to powerful officials. But of course, there are nuances to the levels of disgust each of us feels.

This scenario is more closely aligned with our moral and ethical codes than our values, but it is part of that web of things that make us get out of bed with that bounce. For you it may be the thought that you stood your ground and did not give in when a bribe was expected. For me it could be the thought of helping someone realise the true potential of their ideas and paying that bribe. Whatever the factors are that drive us on, that is what we mean by values, in this context. Passion, drive, enthusiasm, or a bounce in your step, these are the things values give you. But now comes the magic. For now, you must demonstrate how these values are aligned with your business aims and objectives.

- How do they fit together?

References

de Koven, B. (2013), *The Well-played Game*, Cambridge, MA: The MIT Press.

Konami Group Corporation mission statement, (2022), https://img.konami.com/ir/en/ir-data/co_download/pdf/all.pdf, (p.3) Accessed 12.01.22

PAC-MAN (1980), https://www.bandainamcoent.com/games/pac-man, Accessed 05.08.23

Rumelt, R. (2011), *Good Strategy Bad Strategy*, London: Profile Books.

Salen, K. & Zimmerman, E. (2004), *Rules of Play: Game Design Fundamentals*, Cambridge, MA: The MIT Press.

3
MISSION

Where the vision statement tended to be more transformative in nature, the mission is more about the purpose of the project. Where the vision was idealistic and expansive, the mission needs to be more grounded in the everyday of the project's operations. It must connect the internal with the external. That means the mission needs to explain the market that the game is serving and then go further by explaining why the game serves this market. This links to the scope and the scale of the project, what is the range of things this game will do in a practical sense (scope), and how much of this can realistically be achieved in the identified market (scale). There is also one more piece of the mission that needs adding, the operational steps that will be taken to achieve these ideals.

It may be the case that some projects will view the mission as more importantly weighted than the vision because of the practical nature of this chapter. It also tends to codify the values of the project founders more implicitly. This is a natural combination and when we use the term implicit, we are not promoting the idea that the culture is so hidden that readers need to be detectives to uncover these. A good mission section has the ideals, and, the desires, of the project founders embedded in this section. These reflect the purpose of the project, the goals of the project, and the values that guide the project and enable it to fulfil the mission to a standard that is appropriate given the research and analysis conducted on the condition of the market.

We can see therefore that the mission is far more grounded and practical. It reflects what will be the strategy for the game to succeed, whatever success may look like. But as with the vision, crafting a good mission section takes time to write, reflect, and mature into something that can be useful both internally as a focus for the team and externally as something that helps those less familiar with the project to see the 'how' and 'why' of the game in much more focus.

DOI: 10.1201/9781003352594-3

The reader can have different expectations depending on their motivation for reading the business plan. An investor might be looking at the project as something that can add value in pecuniary terms. They may have a shorter-term view of the project and that is how they will read the mission, looking for clues about these elements. But contrast this with a publisher, these people may read the project as a contribution to their portfolio. It must sit alongside their existing games they have previously brokered a deal with. In this case the publisher would have quite a unique way to view the claims made in the mission. It is the same text, but because motivations differ, they have diverse ways to read the statements you craft.

You must be bold and remember that not every investor, publisher, or member of a team is going to have the exact same opinions about the project. It is important to take the time to craft the statement. But it is equally important that the drafts and final statement are not overly subservient to the paradigms of any group(s). The mission must reflect the true purpose of the project as you, the founder and developer, see it to be. For most games, this will not be a major issue, but for the game that seeks to push limits and challenge conventional thinking, this becomes more of a focus. As these paradigms get challenged, this can create friction and lead to a situation where the game needs stronger justification and the quantification of the game's metrics need to be clearly stated.

History has many such games that were there to challenge society or paradigms [hover over for explanation 01 PARADIGM] of a particular group. Many failed and are now lost to the victory of time. But some do breakthrough and lay a challenge for the CUPs who are brave enough to test the value in these games and engage with them. This is not the place to list such games (but if you need some guidance on the type of game meant here, look at the history of Monopoly or Slave Tetris to get a feel of this kind of challenge). The point is that the paradigm assumptions about the way the world works is always reflected in the games we produce. No matter the issue being used as either focus or backdrop, the make-up of your background and the assumptions you have about the world is where your paradigm lies. It is a constructed reality that you have brought to the game. It is your mission to achieve, on your terms. That is super important to remember. Because if you have a game that matters, something important to say and play, then you will attract opposing views. Some of those will need engaging with. Deciding which ones to engage can be problematic depending on the topic under discussion and the level of heat in any arguments that unfold.

Again though, this reminds us that we have choices. Not just about the type of game we want to produce, but about what we want to prioritise in the development of that game. We have a choice over what gets included and excluded in our mission statement. This statement will tell the world where our priorities lie. They explicitly open our concerns and how we want to be accountable for addressing these concerns. Even more important are the strategic choices embedded in this statement. For this is also where we tell the world what strategic parameters we want to operate by. Where we see the boundaries of our strategy marked out and how we will operate within these confines. What gets mentioned in this statement acts as a quality signal to the readership. It confirms that these things are important enough to be part of the strategy that will enable the game to thrive in the market while meeting, changing, or extending the paradigmatic view of the sector. Let's look at an interesting mission from Stonemaier Games.

3.1 Stonemaier Games Mission Statement

We strive to bring joy to tabletops worldwide through memorable, beautiful, fun games. Our games seek to capture the imaginations of all types of people, as our goal is to build games and communities that include experienced gamers, new gamers, solo gamers, partners, larger groups, people of all ethnicities, genders, creeds, cultures, nations, sexualities, abilities, and ages. Through various content we try to add value to our fellow creators in a way that extends beyond board games by sharing our entrepreneurial successes, mistakes, and insights, as well as our love for a wide variety of games. We also believe in constantly evaluating and improving our creation process to improve the environmental sustainability and accessibility of our games.

We can see how they sum things up. They provide the reader with a snapshot of how the project can be perceived as both a character, but also belonging to the CUP segment that it wants to appeal to. We stated earlier that this is a balancing act that needs careful thought and a fair amount of reflection before you get it right. A balancing act that needs fine adjustments to find equilibrium in the way things are conveyed. It is important because a good mission statement can help to motivate internal teams and external readers into action. This action, of course, is not just a random act of help or kindness, it is nudged by what these people have read in your statement. They can buy into it, and they can see the benefits of doing so.

Very few of us are natural born copywriters. Some of us set out to learn the craft with the sole intention of getting better at it as we progress. But for the majority (including this author), this is a challenging thing to get good at. But no matter the type of personality you regard yourself to be, nor the type of opportunity you have decided to attempt, a good vision statement, well crafted, will take you far. Put simply, it helps define the actions needed with the values in the culture of the project. This alignment can help you draw more from the people involved in the project at many levels because they can clearly take on board where it wants to go and why it wants to achieve these things.

This can also be problematic. We still need to make the pitch to 'sell' the project (internally or externally). That means we may have to quantify things that are difficult to quantify. In the example above, we saw the term 'joy' in Stonemaier Games vision. But how do you think a big corporation like Stonemaier Games could measure joy? If you are in a class today, do a quick survey, what do your peers think 'joy' is? How would they measure how joyful they were while having breakfast this morning?

Some of these people may be able to think back to the time they ate their breakfast and reflect on how they felt, getting up, making their breakfast, and then consuming their breakfast. Most people will not have an issue answering this question, even those who do not eat breakfast but have a glass of fruit or vegetable juice would be comfortable answering the question. They can recall with some accuracy their experiences that morning. They can express a subjective opinion about their morning. But for others this will be a challenge. They may have difficulty accurately recalling the morning and the experiences they encountered, the feelings of happiness they felt, could equally be difficult to recall. Some people may not have difficulty answering the question but may not be genuine with you about their experiences. This should always be borne in mind when doing your research (see Chapter 5).

Equally, the breakfast may have been delightful, but if they then experienced a stressful situation, it may affect their recall of the morning experience. Imagine if breakfast was fine but they then missed their bus. This may impact the entire reflection on their morning.

Exposure to explicit dangers is also a real possibility. If you have no track record or are attempting to change things in existing paradigms, you are a challenger and therefore open to criticism. Not least from the parties that you challenge. History is full of failed rebellions from both political and cultural perspectives. If your game is going to challenge homogenised values of a particular group, then you better be prepared for a backlash.

In these rare but important instances, your mission statement can be a guiding principle for those that accept your perspective and get onboard with your project. Even for the more conforming game producer, getting the word out there and connecting with interested tribes can be vital to the success of the project. Setting out strategic goals is going to be vital for these groups to understand and accept your project. For commercial and social challengers of any sector, the discourse will need help and support from their tribes. For small game developers, this may well be a bottom-up approach that lends itself well to an exchange of learning and ideas, as emphasised by Kerr (2017).

The mission statement, therefore, needs to be coherent and concise, while balancing this with specific issues and strategies that will enable this project to survive and thrive. That sounds like some romantic and optimistic outcomes of the exercise. In some ways that is intended; you need to understand both the power and the ability to persuade that can be baked-in when you craft vision and mission statements. The difference of course is that this mission statement is based on purpose, why you are doing what you are doing with this project. The mission must reflect the intentions of the project over the next few years. But here we encounter an issue. For the end goal may change as things progress and develop.

This means that the mission may ebb and flow over time. Be aware that this may be a further challenge for the project if stakeholders are aware of these changing positions of purpose. Most projects will only need to make infrequent fine adjustments to better reflect their purpose. But if this is happening more frequently, then maybe the project is responding to a radically changing cultural space and time or the purpose is not as well developed and stated as it should be. Either way, looking back on the statements and how they have evolved can be a useful exercise. Seeing how things have diversified and evolved over time can be useful in thinking about the future. This is especially true when patterns can be seen in the changes made. The patterns themselves may be poor predictors of the future but they do help tell a story about the project and that helps clarify views of the culture, when seen through the lens of purpose.

3.2 Strategy

This section starts with a quote, a very grounded quote that sets the stage for the coming section, that comes from Rumelt: 'The purpose of good strategy is to offer a potentially achievable way of surmounting a key challenge' (2011: 54).

The good news is that you have already identified the crucial steps needed to make the game. Some will need refining, and we will tackle that a little later, but you already have some idea about what the project will be about, a vague(?) recognition of who your CUPs are, and some thought given on how this thing will look in the world, and how the world looks with this thing in it. There is something forming in the way this thing will be brought to life. One more piece of good news, you may not have all the answers to the provocative questions you have asked, but you are, by now, starting to think about the objectives and the purpose of the project.

Together, these things are starting to indicate how the various components fit together and help define the 'why' and the 'what' while starting to meet the needs of the project. Dangers lie in trying to do too much at once. If a simple card game has 1,000 objectives to meet in the next six months, focus will be lost as the motivation of the team starts to dwindle. Rumelt goes on to state 'Good strategy works by focusing energy and resources on one, or very few, pivotal objectives whose accomplishment will lead to a cascade of favourable outcomes' (2011: 53). Again, solid words of wisdom from Richard Rumelt should help you realise that simplifying things should be a priority when starting out on your strategy planning tasks. For most small studios, there will be fewer multiple committees or board members to convince and appease. There should still be varied voices with opinions you respect providing you with critical advice, but this then becomes a localised issue deciding if you accept or reject that input. This can be difficult, for example, imagine a trusted mentor provides advice that you know is good but results in higher levels of pressure on your time, or even a longer projection before profits are realised. It is tough because you must decide on what gets listened to and accepted and what gets listened to and rejected.

Whatever it gets accepted or rejected, it is important that the goals fit into the overall focus of the project and to see where the diverse levels of objectives impact the project. Campbell et al. (2002:18) helpfully define the categories for impact into three levels: strategic, tactical, and operational. The level with the biggest potential for impact is the strategic level. Decisions at this level are calculated based on uncertainty and they are made with input from the least amount of people. In large organisations, it is a top-down approach, and it sets the path for the entire organisation to follow. For the small games producer too, the effects of strategic-level decisions are based on uncertainty and speculation. It is a centralised set of decisions about where the project is headed and how/when it may expect to get there.

The strategic level is for the long term and will use the ebb and flow of society and the sector the project operates in (that is the paradigm of the sector) to base decisions on. You should be able to see the issue straightaway. The very fact these decisions are based on any paradigm should indicate how off target some of the ideas will be. Entrepreneurs and project managers in any sector are dealing with issues of governance, culture, and markets all at once. These often lead to conflicting perspectives of the world and the nature of how it operates. In these circumstances, it can be easy to forget these forces are present and always in a state of flux. But formulating strategy must take account of these issues from the perspective of management to create the objectives and identify the challenges that will be faced. Strategic levels are therefore more about the longer-term orientation and outcomes.

No one has a crystal ball to tell where the future will take society or what the next paradigm shifts will be. This is where the skills of management are most effective. Good management of the games that get developed, that make it and survive beyond a one-hit wonder are the ones that can take advantage of multiple scenarios of where things are heading in their market and make calculations based on these scenarios. Objectives are then set, and the competitive advantage of the game or studio is understood in the context of these perceived futures (Campbell et al., 2002).

When you start out there will be a substantial number of competing tasks demanding your attention and your money. Deciding where to spend money and concentrate resources is a challenge. It is also one that is very dependent on your individual vision of what success should look like for the project. Learning to cope with the pressure and being able to make decisions that you are confident about is one of the most useful skills an entrepreneur will learn. Being able to make strategic choices is essential in your development as a project founder.

Tactical levels are the second of the three levels. This is where the strategy gets realised in the context of what is going on in the functioning of the game. That is decisions are made on how to meet the objectives that have been developed at the strategic level. For example, these could include the colours of the packaging or the wording in the instructions through to play tests and analysing feedback about the game. These things tend to be more certain and less abstract than the strategic levels that need to be considered, but they also have a direct impact on the meeting of the objectives for the game.

Finally, the operation level. These concern the day-to-day running and result in decisions being made that affect the way things are done that are frequently seen by the customer. Campbell et al. (2002) use the fulfilment of orders as an example. Sending out the right things at the right time to the right people meets a tactical objective that fulfils the holistic strategy of the project's management. It is a simple yet clear demonstration of how these daily procedures, that are often happening right before the customer, and therefore need a degree of transparency, can have a ripple effect in helping to meet the strategy that has been chosen as optimal for the project (see Table 3.1).

Things can change and new data are constantly being processed that can have profound results on our plans. War, social acceptance,

Table 3.1   Levels of Strategy

LEVELS OF STRATEGY		
Strategic	Tactical	Operational

or behaviours previously thought taboo or technological advances all have an impact on how we see the world and the decisions we take against this backdrop. But to reiterate a common theme in this book, these changes are created and maintained by agents like you and me – people that make decisions in everyday life. Future trends are already here; things happening today can lead to swings in behaviour or political decisions that can have a profound effect on the way things are in the future. On a more philosophical note, this affects the very nature of reality and truth. Our episteme and ontology.

Take workplace bullying as an example. In the 1980s, ways of interacting with colleagues were accepted that would be considered an outrage in today's workplace. Jokes and attitudes on sexuality, mental health, race, and disability that may have been brushed off as banter in that era are no longer tolerated to the same degree today. This extends to beliefs of entire sectors; the paradigm shifts over time. But many of these shifts are rooted in things happening right now, in the present. The trick for decision makers is to think about the consequences of these changes. What are the forces driving these things, what does this mean right now for this project, and, more importantly:

- What will be the outcomes for the future of these things?

We started this book by suggesting that the business plan is the greatest piece of fiction you will ever write. Because things are changing and added information is being uncovered, all the time. Therefore, the project can and must adapt to change while presenting the business plan and the strategies therein as something fixed and stable. A clear declaration of where you are and where you intend to go. But the reality of course is that as new things and thinking emerge, the cognition behind the route taken so far with the project may need adjusting in these future scenarios.

This hints at the paradox of running a project. Like building a studio on shifting sand, the integrity of the structure will be impacted more by the movement of the foundational sands. This should be remembered when writing your business plan. Things will change and shift. But the real value in writing a business plan is not in the long-term view it offers, but in the focus, it will provide you as you set out on the project venture and exploration that will undoubtedly lead you to some surprising places. Being able to recognise and then state what the guiding principles are for the project will help provide some stability when things change and fluctuate. Furthermore, business plan writing should provide you with a set of parameters that will help you digest and process information, especially when this information is coming at you in volumes and at speed. By knowing the parameters of what it is you seek, the course of action will be clearer to you.

References

Campbell, D., Stonehouse, G. & Houston, B. (2002), *Business Strategy: An Introduction*, 2e, Oxford: Butterworth-Heinemann.

Kerr, A. (2017), *Global Games: Production, Circulation & Policy in the Networked Era*, Abingdon: Routledge.

Rumelt, R. (2011), *Good Strategy Bad Strategy*, London: Profile Books.

Stonemaier Games mission statement. https://stonemaiergames.com/about/mission-statement/ Accessed: 03.10.2022.

4
OPERATIONS

This chapter is asking for an outline of what things will need doing daily. The focus in this chapter is on the kazillion tasks that will need management's attention every day of the project's existence. These are things that can be planned for. Like renewing software licences or making sure supplies of tea and coffee are sufficient. There are also those things that will require immediate reactions to prevent things from escalating into a more serious situation. For example, neglecting to get insurance cover or letting a deadline slip for account submissions. Time can easily be consumed on tasks that seem to be part of the operations but are things that can wait until an appropriate moment is found for tackling them. Prioritising these things that really cannot wait and making sure the things that really are urgent get done, is key. But the overriding concern when assigning urgency to specific tasks is to reflect on the strategy for the project's success.

* Does completing these tasks help meet the strategic objectives?

This is where operations can become tricky to manage, seeing how they support and feed into the overall strategic objectives set in the previous chapters. That inevitably means comparisons need to be drawn between the real-world impact operations have and the intended impact these things were meant to have on a particular situation or context. Coming back to the vision and mission (Chapters 2 and 3), these operational factors need to be aligned with the general direction of travel and supportive of the overall strategy. Being able to measure these things becomes important and, in this chapter, you will need to outline what and how things will be measured. This means that the vision and mission statements are far from some nice to have, but void of meaning, texts. To be useful, they must mean something directly for the project, they must show where the project will be and what the project will be. Operations must now align by having the

DOI: 10.1201/9781003352594-4 **41**

right team (see Chapter 4.2), the right compliance to do things legally (see Chapter 4.1), and of course controls to ensure the whole thing is on track and not wasting resources (see Chapter 4.3), that will restrict the project's ability to meet its objectives (see Chapter 4.5). Risks associated with the project also need assessing (see Chapter 4.4), which will demonstrate a thorough understanding of the scale of the issues and challenges that the project may face.

In the paragraph above, we start to get a feel for how wide the remit of this section is. It may seem a dull section to think about and write, but as we start to unpack the scope of these varied operations, we start to get a feel for the scale of the tasks that need consideration and how they can help support the project with attention to prioritising and planning. Things will, in all probability, go awry at times. Some of these things will be out of your control and some things you just will not see coming until it is too late. But the value here is often in the hindsight these events provide. This brings us full circle to the fact that not everything can be predicted. More than this, insight based on solid research and findings can provide you with ideas for the planning of the operations, and it is here, in this planning, that the real value of this section of the business plan becomes more evident. It has potential for impact throughout the project's life span and is a chance to demonstrate to the reader how the operations will support the overall guiding strategy for the project.

As mentioned, this inevitably means being able to measure the outcomes of the daily activities in the operations helping management understand where the project is in comparison to where it should be. The difference should not be too significant with the project more on course than not on course. This is the point in being able to measure things. Those things are the desired direction of travel for the project compared with the actual direction of travel. In many ways, these things reflect the kind of organisational culture you have created. The very fact these things are measured and reflected on is a statement about the kinds of procedures and the methods for getting stuff done around your project. The question then of course is:

- What are these *things*?

Let us imagine your board game needs producing and packaging. You estimate sales increasing steadily at first and then the sales pace

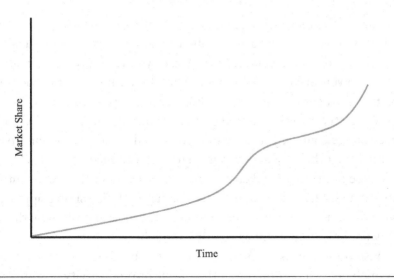

Figure 4.1 Market share over time.

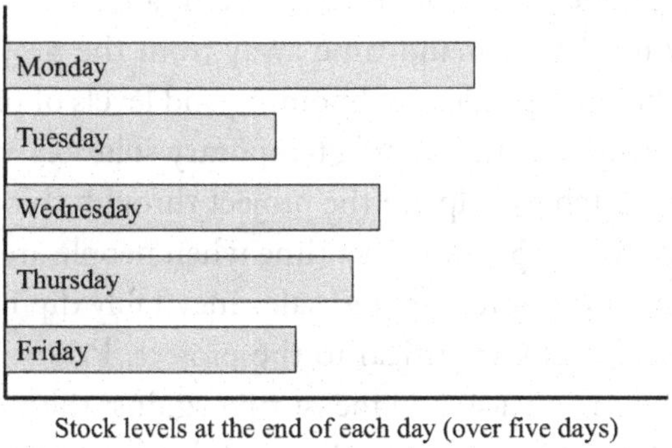

Stock levels at the end of each day (over five days)

Figure 4.2 Daily stock levels.

speeding up as more people get to hear about it and the demand increases (Figure 4.1). Through the research you have done, you are able to say with confidence what the volume of market share looks like for your board game with increasing market share over a period.

This has given you a precise set of numbers to work with and reflect on. On a daily basis, you could keep track of how many resources have been used and what stock levels are left; weekly, this could provide a useful picture of the stock levels (Figure 4.2).

At the same time, you could do the same with sales, providing you with a practical insight into the units being produced, the stock levels you have, and the sales being made. It provides you with a clear picture of the movement of products against the sales. Compare this with the predictions you made about where you want to go against the reality of where you are. It can help you reflect on the situation and help you make decisions about what to do. It could, for example, be that the board game is not selling as well as predicted, so you may decide to try a fresh marketing strategy in a particular locale. Or if your budgets allow, you start to increase online advertising and paid content that the project puts out there on social media.

These decisions are taken based on the operations that are quantifiable and visible. There are really two issues with this simple approach though: (1) things may not be immediately visible and (2) these things may not be as important as you first thought.

Visibility is an issue because there may be times when sales (for example) have a natural dip in their cycle or productivity of staff goes down because of something that cannot be foreseen. Health is an obvious one; people may have to take care of a relative or themselves and suddenly need to demand time away from the project, resulting in slower production. If sales are booming and levels of production are critical to meeting demand, then a temporary solution will be needed as a temporary patch to help see the project through this period. Then again, imagine this happening in a time when people are traditionally on holiday, say in the summer, and sales inevitably dip in this period; then, perhaps, this is less critical to the project. Prioritising helps us see when things are critical and measuring against these observations, the quantification of results of trading will lead to better insights and more rational decisions.

Once again you should be able to see this also reflects the culture of the project. It is a question of how things are dealt with – not just complying with regulatory requirements but also a question of empathy towards the situation, critical or not. It is about how things get prioritised and what this represents to the people you work with. Even the very fact there are policies to measure things daily tells us something about the culture of the project. Some people might see surveillance techniques that make them feel uncomfortable. Others might see it as deeply inspiring as management having their finger on the pulse of the project with clear plans and ideas about growth for the project's future. These people might translate this as a secure project that they are happy to be associated with. The surveillance for them is a payoff and means longevity in terms of their work and continued professional development.

But of course, there is a central question that we have not tackled yet:

- What is it you are going to measure?

The next few pages will provide some insight into the more generic areas that need to be controlled and measured. But each project and each game are a unique combination of variables that result in the character of the culture. This means that your business plan may want to change headings around, not include some, add additional ones, or reword things to better suit your ideas. Never be afraid of making your own mark on these things, each plan is different, and the writing process should reflect this uniqueness in your thinking, because it is your thinking. It can help the reader better define the special qualities of your project and the strategy you have decided to pursue that will lead to the success you envision, whatever that may look like in your context.

4.1 Compliance

We live in a society with civic and civil duties assigned to us. Civil and civic well-being are therefore important for a flourishing society. It also means having responsibilities to ensure the continuation of this well-being. Acting fairly to other members of our society is just one way we do this. Society is a wide association and specific debates about what exactly a civil society should be is open for debate. This is not the place for these debates to be voiced but this is the place, as part of the author's civil duties, to raise awareness of the concept of civil well-being and implications for the games you want to develop. Following Morris (2012), the implications we will be focused on in this section comes in three distinct forms: carelessness, recklessness, and negligence. Each one can materialise in many varied forms, but in this chapter, we will contextualise why these are important with simple examples. The point to remember is that even with simple games, there may be compliance issues that need to be addressed.

For the small game's producer, an example of carelessness would be not correcting an element of the game that was highlighted to the developer in playtests. An obvious example is the use of small counter pieces that look like sweets and appeal to children. It is a legal requirement that a warning should be conveyed on the packaging. Not complying would be reckless. The lack of action is an issue and may have profound consequences if a child, adult, or even animal was injured. Likewise, certain chemicals are not allowed in inks used for the printing of cards or packaging; again, not checking these things is *careless*, not taking action to comply with the legal stance of the civil code is *reckless*.

An accusation of negligence is a more serious outcome that should be avoided. This can result in a loss of reputation or legal procedures that can have devastating consequences for the project. To prevent any of these circumstances from becoming a reality, we have laws, a set of rules and standards that we must comply with. At times, simply trying is not enough, there are some standards that must be met by agents in a society. The sanctions for those that fail can mean their projects being halted or companies dissolved. In the extreme, prison sentences can be issued to those found responsible for *negligence.*

Compliance is therefore important in a civil society. In England, the Trading Standards body acts to regulate and enforce standards and compliance. The range of issues they deal with can be for far-reaching concerns that businesses or consumers have. This will concern an organisation acting unfairly or plainly breaking the law. It is important that standards are met to ensure consumers are not sold dangerous, faulty, or fake products. Even products sold and then found to be substandard, because promises are made in advertising the products that are then not met, can be brought to the Trading Standards attention. If the issue is with advertising per se, then the Advertising Standards Authority and the Committee of Advertising Practice are independent regulatory bodies. Another area both bodies can aid consumers is when unethical procedures are used to pressure CUPs into either playing or purchasing a game against their better judgement.

A further example can be found in the video game sector. Loot boxes have been the focus of past campaigns highlighting the perception that these are perceived as gambling. But this debate is countered from the view that players do receive something in the trade they willingly enter as part of the gameplay experience. Whichever side of this debate you are on, it serves to highlight how things can evolve and change in the regulatory frameworks that we need to comply with over time. Interestingly, one of the first nation states to ban loot boxes was China. One of the biggest games at that time in China was League of Legions (Riot Games, 2009), but with the introduction of the ban, Riot Games were left with a huge hole in their cash flow to consider. Following China, many other states started to insist these game elements were banned. This meant that game developers behind titles using this form of revenue stream had to rethink their strategy and cash flow position. The introduction of this kind of regulation also has another effect that could potentially lead to even greater issues.

Imagine you have produced a successful video game and people all over the world are loving and playing the game. Measuring success in terms of the number of dedicated fan sites, competitions with the game and, of course, revenues are positive. Then the kind of regulatory changes we saw with the loot boxes hit your game. This could mean an entire rewrite of the code, the characters, or even the plot. Changes in the dynamics and mechanics of the game are going to cost you a lot of resources to fix. Management must, therefore, be attentive to even the smallest of suggestions to challenge the model they have used and the changes in the regulatory landscape that could affect their proposition.

From complying with the wording on packaging to being super sensitive to regulatory changes, it's important that the compliance is met, and that the ethical stance of the decisions management take are also considered. This is what I call civil well-being. For not only are you complying with legal requirements but your project is also doing the right thing. By doing the right thing, you may also win over some of the critics you may otherwise have encountered. Reviews from your player base are super important for game developers no matter the scope or scale of your operations. But it should also be remembered that reviewers are often amateurs, not professional critics. They are also sometimes international in their reach and connected with consumer tribes beyond your game genre. If an ethical element of the game helps these critics see the real value or convince them to change their stance towards your game, then these elements are worth highlighting.

It is important to find up-to-date information about what is happening in your market and the kind of changes that are being predicted that will impact your game. The sector-specific press is a good starting source; trading standard bodies often have a news section where their experts and others in the sector discuss potential changes and challenges. For Europeans, the European Union Commission is a reliable source of information. Consultation calls to organisations in member (and sometimes non-member) states can hint at changes on the horizon. Business groups that are more generic can be helpful, such as The Chambers of Commerce or The Federation of Small Businesses for those in the UK. Some firms have up-to-date blogs where they talk about potential changes to regulatory conditions. It should also be remembered that different perspectives can lead to quite different opinions on points of regulation and the expectations for compliance. Compliance can be tricky and fraught with risks (see Chapter 4.4), but it is vital that your team stay up to date and take responsibility for keeping a watchful eye on the regulatory landscape.

One last point on this is that it should also be remembered that personal networks can also be useful sources of information. Regular contact with other people in your field can help you to see a bigger picture and challenge some of your own thinking.

4.2 Team

The team outline is super important for the reader of the business plan. For some external investors, this can be the most important aspect of the business plan and any pitch that gets delivered on the back of it. As an investor, there are three things I look at to help me determine if I shall invest or not. They are the team, the project itself, and the finances. I am not alone either; I know from conversations with other investors that this pattern gets repeated. It may surprise you that people come before the project or the finances, but I like to think there is a simple logic to this approach; if the people are not right or if their record of accomplishment and their presence in the project feels wrong or simply does not add up, then the chances of the project succeeding are reduced. Think about it; if the right people are not on board or in place, then how can the project be expected to make the most of what they have? Ideas are everywhere; innovation is often guesswork. But people are the one thing that will make a project work. People furnish the project with their expertise, tacit knowledge, and networks and soft knowledge capital. Without the right team, things are going to be much harder, and that essential traction, all games need when they launch, is going to be a greater challenge if not missing altogether.

The other side to this coin is the persona and likeability of the main people behind the project. When you meet potential stakeholders, whatever the context, for example, seeking investment or a partnership in some form, these stakeholders must warm to you and your idea. From the perspective of the business plan, it is important to demonstrate a connection with, and track record to, the games sector or the genre of game that you are proposing. For example, imagine the game is a card game to help students remember the names and classification of minerals (we will call it the Serious Mineral Game). Then, there should be some connection between the team to this sector. Whether that connection is in an educational, industrial, or economical context, even faint connections, those that are a little ambiguous, can help to show interest and passion for this sector.

But this section of the business plan is not the place for a full-blown curriculum vitae. If you really want to include this, and it may be requested by some readers, then add this to the appendices at the rear. This chapter should offer the reader a snapshot of the founders, and if appropriate or known, a summary of the rest of the team or the freelancers that will be involved. It is the place to brag a little about past achievements and the connections team members have within the industry. Think about who you know and how you might get an endorsement from them for the project. Whether this is a celebrity or an industry superstar, not really known beyond the confines of the sector, it is always good to highlight these connections. Obviously, the stronger this connection the better, but it is important to be honest and transparent in this chapter of the business plan. It can be tempting to exaggerate the game you last built and how successful it was or the conversation you had with a potential investor who liked the game's idea. But do not over promise on these; the world may feel big, but the games sector can often be tribal and well connected and there is always a chance that the reader/investor of the plan might know the very people you are talking about.

The connections should also show how they provided you with an insight into the sector and this has helped you develop the game idea. Track records can be expansive too. For example, imagine you had been a former salesperson where you proved your ability to sell, or a former air steward that has learned to connect with people and be personable to a wide range of cultures or how to deal with tricky situations (people complaining etc.). These are transferable skills that might help the development of the Serious Mineral Game. As a former salesperson, you know how to gain people's attention and how to manage budgets and, as an air steward, you know how to manage a small team and get the best from the stakeholders of the project. Making these connections visible helps the reader make clearer and more pragmatic connections between the people involved at the heart of the game's development and the objectives that were stated earlier in the vision and mission chapters above. These experiences add to the richness of the team and the skills they bring to the project but of course, they must be relevant to the game. When you talk about these, be concise about the skills and make these coherent to the vision being suggested in the business plan.

There is one other aspect to this Chapter and the reason why the team is important. It brings us back to the paradigm we discussed earlier; this chapter is a good opportunity to explain that the founders get the industry and understand how (at some levels) it operates. For the reader, this industrial insight builds confidence as they can more readily make connections between the vision, management, and the past experiences these people have had that has given them these insights for the game. One way to build on this is to be explicit about the roles that each member of the team will play and how these build on their past experiences. If the members have been working together before, especially on developing a product of some kind, then this adds value for the plan; again, it is all about a demonstrable track record. Even when past schemes have failed to realise their goals, there was surely some knowledge capital gained that can add value to this new project.

4.3 Resources

To be able to create the game you want to create:

- What do you need to enable this to happen?

This is a fundamental question to anyone trying to get a game out there in the real world. But for the game's developer, this also comes as a double-edged sword. The project needs resources to get to market, but the game itself may also need resources for the player to use during game play experience. This chapter, in fact this book, is not about how you go about developing a game but it is about the business case for the game and how you might write a business plan to cement the idea. Neither is this chapter about to offer you a definitive list of resources you will need. Every game is different and will require specific things to help get to the market it requires.

Things purchased to help make the game need to be used in some way to create a higher value than the original expenditure. These are the resources you need, and they all need to be carefully considered. From the computer you use, the pens you use, the books you read, subscriptions you sign-up to through to the people that help you. All are resources and all need sourcing from somewhere. Things can shift too; for example, if you need a specialist, high-quality printer to print boards for a mock-up of a potential board game, which will be used only a limited number of times, it may not be justifiable to purchase a high-end printer when you are still testing and developing your game. This specific service can be sourced from elsewhere and brought in as a third party (outsourced). Not all assets can or should be owned and controlled by the project. Borrowing or hiring these resources can help free up both cash and time, two of the most important resources for any new venture. Control is the key in this. For the game to be made, management has a need to control certain resources. That is why we began this chapter with the question we did. According to Osterwalder & Pigneur (2010: 35), in Business Model Generation, these resources are categorised as either physical, intellectual, human, or financial.

To help in the business planning process, it might help to break down those things you need into one of these four neat categories as shown in Table 4.1.

There are issues and challenges to consider in this too. An overview of the most pressing issues is provided in Table 4.2 for a small game's designer to consider.

Whatever the resources for the project, they need to be able to deliver something of value to the project. They may also be a promised

Table 4.1 IP Resource Taxonomy

RESOURCE CATEGORY	EXAMPLE THINGS TO CONSIDER:
Physical	• Places to sell • Software for creating code or digital assets • Secure storage (both physical and digital) • The studio you work in
Intellectual	• IP in the game/for the project • Data sets built for play tests • Terms and conditions of suppliers
Human	• Marketers • Sales force • HR • Anyone relied on to help create the game • Your CUP segmentation etc.
Financial	• Cash in the bank • Runway length • Investors (in all forms)

resource that is yet to be delivered on. Financial support is a good example; imagine a financial institution has agreed to a line of credit that is yet to be accessed. The line of credit will need repaying and will come at a cost for the project. They are also controlled and governed by the lending institution. It is always advisable to avoid debt when possible and limit the exposure of the project to these instruments. There is also the need to plan for unexpected situations when the cash flow may take a downturn. Or imagine having to turn business away because the revenues generated are attractive, but the profit margins on this activity are so small that it is simply not worth pursuing. The resources you have available would be better used on another, more profitable (even if less revenue generating), assignment? It does happen and without some sort of plan, the project is going to suffer in these situations, terminally.

Likewise, the guarantees from investors that they promise to buy shares in the company (not the project), at some predetermined date and for a predetermined price needs to be considered as this resource has the potential to fail to materialise if the transaction is not correctly formalised. In most situations, an offer from the company to sell does not oblige the purchaser to take-up the offer. This kind of deal is known as a stock option, and although they are common in business transactions there is, as always, some consideration needed

Table 4.2 Generic Pressing Issues

CATEGORY	EXAMPLE ISSUES AND CHALLENGES TO CONSIDER:
Physical	Physical things do not last forever and while this is often classed as an accounting issue, it can have a major impact on the capabilities of the project. From this perspective there are three issues to consider: i) costs associated with acquiring the asset in the first place. This has obvious implications for the start-up budgets. But then, ii) there is also the cost associated with locating, running, repairing, and insuring these resources. iii) Finally, consider the end of the resource's usefulness in the project. Are these resources of value to others? In which case they may be sold on. Equally though they may need disposing of which can incur costs. Some resources have no residue value nor serve any value to others. Think about a subscription to some software, which cannot be sold on and has no value to others, but contrast this with an old fridge that still works or a used car.
Intellectual	The most obvious for the games sector is the IP that the project can claim. IP can range in terms of the protection it affords a project. From the basic form of copyright to the more complicated and costly patents. Even when protection is claimed, there is a need to be aware that infringements on your protected creative outputs can happen and this may mean legal costs being incurred. If the fight is long, then there may even be reputational damage to the branding of the project. Branding can provide an element of goodwill for the project but if the perceptions of the quality (for example) of the project are damaged, then that goodwill could be seen evaporating as CUPs experiences are below the quality expected. The brand must be trustworthy and if it is not delivering on that trust, then problems will arise in reputational quality. All brands want to be trusted by their CUPs, but this is more salient for a fresh game project that is new to the market. These should be super sensitive to the expectations and perceptions of the CUPs.
Human	Values, purpose, and trust are all important for the project and should be conveyed through the business plan for the reader. But it could be argued that these elements play a more pivotal role in the human category because the agents in the project that become the faces and voices for the CUPs must be able to spread these elements via the communications and touch points they either produce or interact with. The real dangers are that these elements are not really embedded in the project's core. If this is the case, then the agents in the project are less likely to be enthusiastic about these things which has a consequence for external views of the project. This can be further exaggerated when the project reaches growth phases, and the capabilities and departments start to expand. Here, there are real dangers that the core culture of the project can change in ways that are unforeseen and not complementary to the original culture scheme. What is really happening in these circumstances is a lack of understanding of the original values of the project and the original crew that may have been responsible for the codification of these core elements, who are the agents that have done most of the heavy lifting till now and have enthusiasm and empathy with the vision to have carried it this far. Their input may help make the core elements more tangible and real for any fresh agents joining the team. With expansion, more formal training material and programs may be needed to consolidate standards for the project and explain the core elements of the values in the brand and how to translate these. It may also help reaffirm some of the core elements for all internal stakeholders.
Financial	The most pressing issue when starting out is having enough funding to get going with the project (see Chapter 8.2). Game producers' access to funding can be one of the more fundamental barriers to market entry. The bigger the needs of the project (and frequently the vision), the more challenging this aspect can be. The issue is that access to business finance is frequently perceived as riskier for the creative sector than for comparable businesses (United Kingdom 2011, 2022).

prior to any formalised agreements being entered into. There are also compliance issues that will need to be addressed by both parties to the potential deal. These parties may even be internal employees of the project, but either way, as a source of financing, they should be viewed with healthy scepticism.

4.4 Risks

You are undertaking a new venture. One that is yet to prove if the demand you anticipate is there. It is a substantial risk, and it could be that things in the research have been misunderstood or you have been over optimistic about the market's demand for your game. It makes sense therefore to consider and evaluate the risks associated with the vision you want to create. Your game will need to be tested with real people, receive feedback, and then you will need to make decisions based on this input. This means you are minimising certain aspects of the risks associated with the desire for your game by the public. But that is only one aspect of the risk associated with your game.

Entrepreneurs are often associated with risk and seen by some as risk takers, prepared to gamble resources on a perception or hunch. While this is sometimes true, it is more the case that entrepreneurs take *calculated* risks. These are based on hard evidence and practical intelligence. That is the lessons they have learned in life that feed into the way they see the world – their paradigm. The practical intelligence relates to the skill set they have acquired and the tacit knowledge they have gained in their experiences of life. Sometimes called know-how (Baum et al., 2011), practical intelligence is something all of us have. We often use it to solve everyday problems we encounter. This means that we have an inbuilt understanding of some of the issues and concerns that we face in starting out with a new venture, creating a new game, or combining both to produce a new entrepreneurial project (whether for profit or supporting social causes). We understand the basic risks and we can take steps to minimise these.

- But what are these risks?

According to Rae (2007, 110), risk can be classified as including one of the following (note how closely some of these align with the STEEPLE analysis tool).

- Lack of knowledge.
- Economic market stability.
- Technology access and the ability to function as planned.
- Financial budgets being realistic and achievable.
- Competitions likely response to your presence in their market.
- Customers not responding to your offer as predicted.
- Supply chain quality and timelines not as expected.
- Human capital whereby the skill set of the team does not align with the needs of the project.

Can you identify the risk from this list that is most likely to impact your game project? Doing this exercise will guide you in seeing how the risks can expose your start-up to potential failure. For bigger firms, there are two ways to approach the risks they face: oversight and management (Marcouse et al., 2014).

Oversight: An ongoing process where the business owners take on the responsibility for assessing what could go wrong and how to mitigate against these factors. This is an iterative process of review. This review means identifying, prioritising, and managing the risks that could have the biggest impact.

Management: Having in place detailed codified procedures and policies for the team to follow should the risk become a tangible reality.

Looking at risk in the context of the above probably makes it look quite daunting. It is. But not taking the risks inherent in starting a games business into account means that the venture, your project, could be exposed to more uncertainty. Planning is the key to managing risk. But putting in place plans for both thinking about risk and strategically calculating the risks you are most likely to encounter will help you build better ventures. So, although oversight and management are often associated with bigger, more established firms, there is no reason why you cannot adopt the same principles in your planning.

Going to a financial institution, of any description, for money to help build your enterprise will be viewed much more favourably if they can see that you have taken the risks seriously and have drawn plans for dealing with these things when, and if, they happen. It adds weight to your project and shows that you have analysed these factors and not tried to avoid them.

Breaking these down even further, Rae (2007) asks readers to consider if the risks are controllable or uncontrolled. You want to be in control. Controlling the risks you may face means developing a plan for those risks. Thinking about how likely the risk is to occur and what planning should be in place, should the risk become a reality. Identifying the risks most likely to become an exposure for the venture means insurances can be put in place to help mitigate some of the impact these could have. The higher the impact the risk is likely to have on the project's ability to function, then the more attention should be given to that risk.

When we focus on the smaller game developer, a key area of risk is in the decision process. How you make decisions has a major impact on the outcomes for the games you produce and the venture behind them, including the likelihood of the business surviving. It makes sense, therefore, to understand both the risks consequences and the returns that the decision will yield for the project. This means taking an active approach to risk and making decisions about how to identify what form a risk may materialise as, when this risk is most likely to occur, and what options are available to help overcome the situation.

Aside from the obvious financial risks inherent in starting up a new venture, the intention in this chapter is to show that risk comes in many forms but can be managed and planned for. Anticipating risks should be a key part of the entrepreneurial process. Risks exist in all of life. Accepting this means that entrepreneurs in the games sector can start to think through their options and get help from others in their assessment of risks and help create a list of actions to help overcome these negatives. A positive outcome of this is that the culture being formed around the vision, and the building of the enterprise, may be one that understands these risks and takes an active role in identifying and measuring these aspects. This will help to control risk as early protocols and systems become embedded in the development of the project from the outset.

An early mapping exercise is a good start to highlight which risks are perceived as most likely to occur and of course their impact. It might also be worth considering if these risks are internal or external. The more understood these potential risks are, the better the planning will be to help overcome them. Sometimes, we also talk about the *appetite for risk*, a very generic term which means the level or tolerance for risk that management are happy to accept. Every project is different and even within the games sector there are quite different attitudes to risk depending on the market the project operates within. But no matter the type of games being produced, measures to try and safeguard against risk can only be taken once the forms of risk are understood and their likely impact or severity on the enterprise considered.

All this must be considered in the context of the returns that can be expected when we take risks. There is an old saying that sometimes the greatest risk is doing nothing. There is always an opportunity cost associated with risk taking; therefore, a sensible assessment of the situation can help to determine if the risk is worth taking. It also means being aware of, and monitoring, the danger signs for risk. For example, a partner is reported in the media to be in financial difficulties, but they have said nothing to you, might suggest the time is right for probing a little about the partners situation and as a safeguard, seeking a new supplier or at the very least starting talks with other suppliers.

Below we offer two tools for measuring, assessing, monitoring, and managing the impact of risk. The first one (Table 4.3) is about the likely impact of this risk and your ability to control the factors associated with it. You must aim to control the space and the potential impact this risk may have on the project. The most dangerous area is the top right, where you have no control over the risk, and it is perceived as possibly having a major impact on the project.

The second tool (Table 4.4) looks at the impact and probability of the risk occurring. Again, the biggest danger is in the top right quadrant.

Table 4.3 Risk Control

LIKELY IMPACT OF THE RISK	HIGH		
	MEDIUM		
	LOW		
	FULL	SOME	NONE
	Control over the risk		

Table 4.4   Risk Likelihood

LIKELY IMPACT	HIGH			
OF THE RISK	MEDIUM			
	LOW			
	MINIMUM	LOW	MEDIUM	HIGH
	Likelihood of the risk happening			

To help visualise ways to see the dangers, some projects will choose to label each category on a Likert scale of one through to five, where one is the lowest and five the highest category of risk. Alternatively, some projects will use words to emphasise the need to assess the risk at intermittent periods. This could range from:

- Review, setting specific periodic evaluations of the risk, e.g., every quarter.
- Monitor, doing a more regular evaluation, e.g., every month.
- Alert, an even more intense evaluation, e.g., weekly.

These are suggested ways to monitor and evaluate the risks you have identified; ultimately though, it is your decision on the level of impact risks have and how best to ensure they have been considered and are not going to suddenly create a critical sudden shock for the project.

4.5 Controls

Any business plan will make significant claims about the impact its aims and objectives are going to have on their market, based on the research they have done and the logical conclusions the authors can deduct from this evidence. In writing the business plan, one of the most salient tasks is to pinpoint this impact and convey the quantified outcome through the document (normally written text). This demands control.

If the business plan overstates this impact and suggests changes to the fabric of society or a radical new form of business modelling, then the plan may come over as too ambitious, especially if the team has no track record in achieving these sorts of ambitions. It may be the case that these changes are feasible, but these kinds of claims must be based on solid insights. Key questions here are:

- How will your game contribute to these changes in attitude?
- How will things be measured?
- At what point will the team, or any stakeholder, recognise progress being achieved towards these aims and objectives?

It should be obvious that there is a need for measurement on which speculation and reality of performance can be compared. Think of this as a safety net for the control of the project. At no point will the project be without direction because the predefined factors for measurement can be used. The best benchmarks are the milestones that will be reached on the journey to getting this game to market and then watching for steady growth. Milestones are good as they add clarity on the performance of the project and are easily understood. Control factors used by the team can help increase buy-in from stakeholders. Both internal and external stakeholders can influence milestones, but balance is needed to ensure these do not create friction with the values of the project. The precise performance indicators chosen are down to the authors of the business plan and the projects team. This is your construction and your impression on these stakeholders to make.

For social projects, this can present an even more acute set of issues. For commercial projects, things can be straightforward to comprehend for the reader, for example, they more readily find utility in, and recognise, revenue and profit as convincing and useful milestones for the projects control. For the social project, these can be opaquer. Anheier (2005: 190) makes a case for the use of program evaluation, where goals are established to help evaluate the impact the project is having in the arena that the intervention is seeking to support. It is important to bear in mind that the situation prior to any intervention is accounted for. This provides the project with a benchmark against which impact can be measured.

As Anheier (2005) emphasises, this is an outcome-oriented method of measuring the impact. Benchmarking tends to be more comparative in this outcome; it helps by stating where the project is against predetermined milestones. A direct comparison can easily be made, and this helps guide the team in making decisions about either staying as they are (no adjustments necessary) or making changes. Change can be either subtle or dramatic depending on the consequences of the insights gained and the interpretation by management.

Novice teams might find Watson's (1993) advice helpful when deciding on what indicators to use as quantifiable criteria when exploring the benchmarking process. These criteria are measured internally, externally, or as a mix of these.

Internally can be the simplest set of criteria to measure as the project management has access and control over this information. For example, comparing sales against advertising and marketing expenditure, or the cost of production against sales, or the efficacy of the game as self-reported by the CUPs. This data is internally produced by the project and is exclusively focused on this specific game in a specific context.

External measurements can be in many forms. We start with a direct comparison of the competition. It can be tricky to compare things the competitor does not want to share, but there are plenty of visible criteria that can be used. For example, are they hiring more staff? To what roles? In what location? When will they be interviewing? All this can tell you things about their future strategy.

It is even possible to draw conclusions and make comparisons with the sector more broadly. For example, trade bodies like Ukie (UK Interactive Entertainment) publish resources that are useful in this regard. Take, for example, their UK Games Industry Census, which highlights general trends in the industry across the UK. Kickstarter is another useful resource; it provides stats on the different sectors that can provide a handy overview.

Another broader mixed method extends the analysis of the market even further and takes account of all the related activities being conducted in unrelated sectors. For example, a small games studio may look at an independent content publisher for comparative purposes. The publisher may be using a strategy or model in ways unusual to the game studio. These insights might benefit the games studio especially if they adopt and adapt these to suit their situation.

Control is vital. Without controls in place, the best strategies in the world are going to struggle to keep going in the short to medium term. This is not about the need to convince external stakeholders that they can have confidence in the project and the team. It is also about the team genuinely seeking the strengths and the weaknesses in the project. These are sometimes subjective and biased but then become more objective as and when they get codified as a business plan. That is because measurements are taken and the need to take further action (or not) is fully understood. The key questions are:

- Are milestones being reached?
- Are these within the timeframe we predicted?
- If not, then what needs to be done to get things back on track?
- What form should change take?
- Could it be that the milestone was wrong and unachievable in the first place?

Hindsight is a wonderful gift. Once data is collected, looking back becomes much more effective to view how things progressed over a period. Right now, for the business plan to be effective in communicating these control tools, it is necessary to outline the milestones in quantifiable terms. That is the milestones to be measured on something tangible in the market. The result, financial figures being assigned to the milestones. These can add clarity for the reader of the plan and help to show how activities that need a lot of resources (including time) can be worthy of pursuit in the longer term.

References

Anheier, H.K. (2005), *Nonprofit Organizations: Theory, Management, Policy*, Abingdon: Routledge.

Baum, J.R., Jean Bird, B. & Singh, S. (2011), The Practical Intelligence of Entrepreneurs: Antecedents and a Link with New Venture Growth, *Personnel Psychology*, 64, 397–425.

Marcouse, I., Anderson, P., Black, A., Machin, D. and Watson, N. (2014), *The Business Book*, London: Dorling Kindersley Limited.

Morris, M. (2012), *A Practical Guide to Entrepreneurship: How to Turn an Idea Into a Profitable Business*, Basingstoke: Kogan Page.

Osterwalder, A. & Pigneur, Y. (2010), *Business Model Generation: A Handbook for Visionaries, Game Changers and Challengers*, Hoboken, NJ: John Wiley & Sons Inc.

Rae, D. (2007), *Entrepreneurship: From Opportunity to Action*, Basingstoke: Palgrave Macmillan.

United Kingdom (2011), *Department for Business Innovation and Skills, Access to Finance for Creative Industry Businesses*, London: Crown Copyright.

United Kingdom (2022), *United Kingdom Interactive Entertainment & University of Sheffield, UK Games Industry Census*, London: Ukie.

Watson, G.H. (1993), How Process Benchmarking Supports Corporate Strategy, *Planning Review*, 21(1), 12–15.

5
RESEARCH

For some people, the research aspect of the plan will be terrifying, reminding them of their school days when learning was forced on them when they only wanted to be playing games. Forms of research are remarkably diverse, but they are all fed by a need-to-know. Research is as diverse as the questions that get asked. This chapter does not offer a definitive list of research methods (the tools you can use to do research) or methodologies (the strategy you can employ to conduct your research). There may be innovative approaches to the research you want to conduct or there may be more traditional routes you want to explore. Either way, the process is important because it will always involve some form of data gathering, analysis, and conclusion. The most pressing rationale for doing research into your game and the market you expect to operate in is to understand something of the creative output you have created.

This also indicates for the game builder the two sides of the same coin this all involves. On one side, research needs to be able to explain how a game works and where the strengths and weaknesses of the concept are found. On the other hand, there is the need to make the business case for this game and this requires a distinct set of data that can help you focus much more on the fundamentals of the market you wish to operate in. The two are complimentary. Playtests will tell you much more about the game and provide greater insights into the real value players feel they gain. These are the benefits they get when playing or even take away with them post-game. These insights will also feed into the marketing and promotion of the game. These are concrete experiences that demonstrate real things people felt they gained. From being happier, learning something, or becoming more productive, it is important to follow up with the players after the tests have been conducted. Players may report not remembering having played the game, which tells you something. Equally, players fizzing

 DOI: 10.1201/9781003352594-5

with enthusiasm and spreading the news about the game also tells you something about the game. Vastly different outcomes, but each tells you something unique about the game.

On the other side of this coin is the need to know the scope and scale of the market, or markets, you think the game will be best suited to. There may be multiple markets that have an interest in this game. This is the customer side of the coin. Even with social games, or games given away for free, it still requires a financial basis on which it can be sustainable. Think of this scenario as a good vampire. Sucking resources from the donor to do good elsewhere. These donors, I would argue, should still be treated as a customer. They are motivated to help you by funding the project.

At the beginning of the above paragraph, we talked about scope and scale. Scope, in research terms, can be used to find out how diverse the market is. This diversity could include the personas of the individuals that are active in the market or the range of games that exist in this area of the market. Taking this further, it may be necessary to know where the games are based or produced. Geography might even tell you something about the market that had not been considered before or lead to some deeper insight. For the scope it might be that a combination of these things provides the greatest insight. But scale can also be important and may be focused on any of the above, but here, as the name suggests, we are more interested in size. The key question then becomes:

- What size are they?
- Do they cluster?

For example, if the market is based in Greater London, UK, then the size or number or organisations in the interactive entertainment sector is far greater than Northern Ireland. But imagine Northern Ireland producing smash after smash and their small studios are winning lots of recognition in the form of industry awards, it would suggest their region needs attention.

- What are they doing that seems to be working so well?

A simple STEEPLE or SWOT analysis might be able to help, but it needs some deeper research to find out what is really going on there and why their creative output is so good. By deeper research, I mean more than just looking at the games themselves. It might mean a visit to some studios to get a feel for the place and having some conversations with the people founding and running these studios.

Research is divided between two related forms of information; these are primary and secondary sources. Playtests are primary because you, as a researcher, are generating information. This could be taking field notes (e.g., where you take notes on how people react to one another while playing or how often people laugh) or asking people to complete a questionnaire. The other end of this research spectrum is secondary sources. This is the use of content that you have not created yourself. Business reports and academic papers are good examples. The key to using these sources is to ask if you consider them reliable enough to use in the business plan. It is also necessary to keep a record of where these sources were found; in other words, keep the citation for them. This will mean you are able to quickly get back to the sources to check things and offer the reader of the business plan a list of the references handy if they want to check things for themselves.

One crucial point to make when you use secondary resources is that this material was created for another purpose than the one you are using it for. A conference paper was written for a particular conference, not for use in your business plan. There is no problem using this kind of material, but the fact that you are now using it in your business plan means the information is being used for a purpose that may not have been the intended purpose of the original author(s).

Secondary sources are often problematic because of the sheer volume of material that is out there. Sifting through this information can be a daunting task, therefore, being systematic and focused on what the information is that you seek will help keep you on track. It will also help to have some clear questions in mind that you want answers to. It may well be that the questions you pose are already answered somewhere in the masses of information that is already out there in the world. Checking for these answers and starting any research with a review of this information may save you a lot of unnecessary work (bearing in mind not everything you uncover will be useful).

This is really an issue of the methodology you plan to use to gather, organise, analyse, and present the information you have collected. That is the strategy you employ to best serve the project by providing optimal insights into the things you need to know. When deciding on the methodology, most people will choose to deploy a mixed method approach in their research. This means, as the name suggests, using both secondary and primary in some form. A good example would be to start doing some reading around the topic and keeping notes on the things you find (secondary research). Having gathered some insights, you then decide to do a questionnaire and survey a sample of the population (customers, users, or players) to find out more (primary research). This leads you to decide to really get into the reasons people feel the way they do, and so you decide to conduct some in-depth interviews (primary research). These three approaches can be triangulated to demonstrate what you have uncovered, adding some weight to the business plan.

5.1 Data

We mentioned in the section above that there is a need for clear questions to be asked. In part, this is asking you for the 'why' in your research, the purpose of doing this activity and potentially spending some time doing this activity. Knowing this will help shape the kind of questions you decide are important, and the things you need to know, which in turn, shape the kind of research you do. Let us think about some questions to use as an example of what we mean here:

Q1: How many games did studio X produce last year?
Q2: How many people are employed in the game sector in my county?
Q3: What are the motivations for people working in the games sector?

Question one (Q1) is straightforward to answer. We can look at Studio X's catalogue or on their web site and find the answer. Q2 is also straightforward to answer, but there are more layers to this question. In Q1 we can quite quickly decide on what we will class as a game, and we can find out with relative ease and a light touch the quantity of games produced. We do not need to know how successful these games were, what kind of genre of game they were, how long each game took to develop, or how many people were involved in the production of the games. We only need a simple number to satisfactorily answer this question.

Question two (Q2) requires a bit more work to answer. Depending on where you are located and what kind of access you have to local government data, it might be more difficult than you initially thought to find answers. But here too there are many nuances to the question. Definitions will be needed to establish exactly what you mean by terms like *employed, game sector,* and even *county*. Going deeper, what do we mean by *people*? How will these agents be defined?

- By age?
- By income?
- Location?

This should begin to demonstrate that the type of question you ask is going to shape the kind of research tools you use to get answers. It may even be necessary to do more than one research project before satisfactory data is uncovered. The way you decide to go about finding answers and recording your findings will be either structured or unstructured. Some literature you read on the topic of data collection will make more granular differences between the types of data collected. For our purposes, we only need to consider the more baseline types of data. Q1 above was easy to answer, we do not need a highly structured approach to gain a sufficient answer. It should be robust enough to use the resources we mentioned above (catalogue and website). As Q2 may require a level of structure, what are you going to plan to do to gain a satisfactory answer? This planning is structured and relates to the kind of question being asked to gain some form of data. Q3 is different.

Whereas secondary sources would suffice for Q1 and Q2, primary may be needed to find data to answer Q3. This means you produce your own data to answer the question. It can be argued that this kind of data generation (primary) often leads to more robust data sets being uncovered. But context, to any research, is important. A structured approach may well produce better data to answer Q3, it may be that it also reveals more questions that need to be addressed and more research that needs to be conducted before any useful data are found. In the planning phases, it is essential that you think about the type of data you are likely to need and the sources of this data. Philosophical arguments around this are not going to be considered here. We do not have the space. This is intended as a lighter introduction to the general themes of research and the most pressing issues for small gaming projects.

- But what do we mean when we talk about data in this context?

We mean any source of information that can be used to address your questions. That is a very wide range of sources that may be found in an equally wide range of places. Being creative in locating these places can be helpful as paradigms get broken down and things looked at from different angles. This can be challenging as accepted views of things are questioned. But it can equally bring fresh thinking and ideas that may not have been visible otherwise.

For the reader of your business plan, it is about having faith that the questions you have decided to ask and the data you have used to make sense of a situation and find answers are a good match. The analysis of this data thus becomes relevant as this will provide some assurances that the research has been conducted thoroughly and logically. The reader will be less concerned with the arguments that pertain to different methodologies. They want to know what questions were asked, how you went about getting answers, and what these answers told you.

- How did these answers guide your decision-making process?

That is important as this is the relatable bit on the operational strategy you focus on for the delivery of the project. Use plain English in this section. Clarity is needed, be clear about what the data consisted of, how you analysed it, and what this told you. If you use statistical software, name it, state the advantages of this software, and move on. Most readers will be far more interested in the results this provided and where it took the project. Likewise for qualitative methods, explain who got interviewed or who was observed playing the game, why they were considered relevant, and what the findings were. More detail can always be provided in the appendices if it adds support for the points being made in the plan.

Justifications in this section are purposefully limited, it is the answers which are often more important to the reader than how the interrogation was conducted. The data is the evidence which can be used in all areas of the business plan. Data act as the bedrock on which much of the rest of the plan gets built. Therefore, an outline of the data is important to the entire business plan but remember to avoid too much detail unless this has been requested (e.g., when the business plan is for an academic audience).

5.2 Customers

As we learned in Section 1.2, customers are the lifeline to any new venture. Finding them can be tricky for some game producers as the concept of the game may be novel. Any research that you conduct must address the fundamental question of who these customers are for your offer. These people will no doubt be buying into games now, games that are produced by your competitors and this may have an impact on your ability to attract these people and persuade them to try your offer. In most sectors, this is straightforward in that you make a product that serves the customer better than the existing offer and you communicate these benefits to them to sell. But with games, the customer may not need to stop playing the games they already have and maybe more inquisitive as to what is on the market. Persuading these types of customers to try your offer is a less challenging thing to do than trying to persuade management in the NHS to try your serious game for their patients or training needs.

But in many ways, this is also to your advantage. Larger studios, creating more expansive games that may serve these needs, are going to have to be planned and managed tightly. They may view the solution these clients need as a distraction from their core business and not worthy of their attention. But as a smaller independent studio, this is the opportunity you can fulfil. For the larger studios, the idea that this game generates small revenues might mean they are dissuaded from trying to satisfy this demand, the revenues and the profits are simply too small for them. But for a smaller studio, hungry to get out there in the real world with their game, to demonstrate that they can add value in some way, this is a huge window of opportunity. One that will give the smaller provider kudos and credence for being the ones to produce this game.

This matters to customers because they can see that others have benefitted from the game, you can state this in the marketing materials you produce, and these new customers can see that the original customers were satisfied. That they got the game when promised, to a quality that was promised and to a standard of game play that was promised. But there is also a further knock-on effect of this for your suppliers. They can see that this is a good outfit to do business with, there is trust to be built, and there is no better way to start building that than with a bunch of satisfied customers to brag about. Suppliers are important for several reasons, but not least because they may be able to offer you terms that help you get going with the project. That is, they can offer extended or more favourable conditions for doing business with them. Or they may be able to offer you some form of sponsorship or connect you to other suppliers you need to consider in the development and commercialisation organizationtion of the game, if that is a route you are taking.

Finding these first few customers is vital for all the above reasons but equally because it will validate your hunches as a project leader and build confidence among the team that you have been able to cre-ate a product that benefits people. Equally important though is the personal touch with these first few customers. They are the ones that have spent money on your game and so it is here that learning can happen that could be pivotal in you continuing with the status quo of the project's offer or making a shift to something fresh.

Customer feedback is essential but along with this is the need to be able to listen to what they have to say and make rational judge-ments based on this input. All touch points these people have with the game, and interactions you have with these people, represent a chance to learn about their needs and wants. Being able to take on board what they are telling you will mean that the communication strategies and the whole idea of who your customers are may change as you learn more about the market. Different methods of interaction should also be tried; we have learned that this means finding the optimal chan-nel of communication and being open to what people tell you. Your assumptions may be right, for example, your customers do prefer to chat with you via online chat functions on your website, but equally, they may prefer to meet you in person and talk to real people about the game and the benefits they got from it. Either way, do not forget to find out from them about the problems they face and what they think could make this game even better.

One word of warning before we conclude this section: some games are bought on impulse. That can mean they are lower-value items bought impulsively. Think about a family on a long road trip, they stop to charge their electric vehicle and buy a travel set of snakes and ladders for the journey. They are not, in these circumstances, going to overthink their choices, they make a snap decision there and then. Packaging and appeal must be persuasive for the family to make the choice of your game over another on the shop shelf. But compare this with the example of the new serious game designed for the NHS, used above in this section. This game has a different customer base and therefore a different type of appeal to that customer. Whereas the snakes and ladders game purchaser is a member of the public, the NHS is a huge organization with set criteria for standards and compliance that must be met before they will consider using you or your game. These are quite different customers that come with vastly different motivations and needs.

Segmenting your customer means being able to identify the distinct types of customers you are going to target with your marketing plans, with common traits they all have. Done properly, it means that you will need to understand the market in all its guises, which, as Ranchhod and Gurău (2007) note, is reliant on external and as well as internal understandings and then grouping all the people identified into suggested categories (see below). In its simplest form, segmenting the customer can be by:

- Demographics (the age of the customer).
- Socio-economic (occupation and income).
- Personality (introvert or extrovert).
- Lifestyle (specific things they do in their life, social video game streamers for example).
- Psychographic (why they are loyal/purchase particular brands).

This is by no means an exhaustive list. By combining these factors, a much better understanding of the customer can be created. When we do this, we create fictional personas of the customer. The key to developing strong customer personas is to do research on the people that buy similar games from your competitors and to then think a little more widely about the consumer tribes (Cova et al., 2011) you may be able to activate and gain as a customer. These tribes may not be customers in your market at present, but they may share a similar problem or have similar interests as the customers your competitors have.

This can get complicated if you are targeting more than one customer group as this will mean the development of several personas to help you understand each one. Even when you only have a single persona to work with, it is always worth naming the persona as this will help you feel greater levels of empathy for the person in real life and it will help prevent stereotypes dominating your persona creation. That is a crucial point as stereotypes are a judgement based on generic and sometimes erroneous ideas about the individuals in a group. The persona, on the other hand, is a very specific piece of research and is always based on concrete findings from the research you have conducted into customers. Bias may still be present in the final configuration of the persona, but this is as objective as you can make it because of the findings you are able to use. Nevertheless, little creativity may be required when creating these personas.

5.3 Market

In the provision of products and services, the need to be economically sustainable is ever present and should be the only question that gets answered right at the start before any energy is expelled on the creation of a plan or a strategy starts to take shape. The bottom line is:

- Can adequate market share be predicted to make the effort worthwhile?

If the answer is negative, then the whole idea of the game shall need careful thought. In short, what you are likely to end up with is a hobby. Which is fine, but most hobbies do not require a business plan.

The contemporary nature of being online first has served to exaggerate this by empowering consumers with the ability to compare and contrast offers from a diverse set of companies in an equally diverse set of geographies. Your consumer is no longer constrained by only local knowledge and understanding. This leads to greater understanding of the differences between competing companies and their offers. It also builds confidence for the consumer that a better deal can always be found by spending a little time searching the Web. It also results in a double standard for you as you enter a market, the data is near endless, and what it really means for your offer can be a fraught exercise. Meeting customers' needs and capturing value from the transaction means locating a market that offers an adequate return on the investment of resources, is more pressing than ever. Part of the issue is not so much a question of how much, how many, or how frequently but the 'what', as in exactly what is in the offer for the purchaser.

To some readers this may seem a bit odd, surely, we know the 'what' of the market. If we are a local based airline flying regionally, then we are an airline, right? Yes, of course. But what market is that airline in? Budget? Premium? Holiday? This matters because the different markets will have distinct characteristics which need considering. Let us imagine our airline is a budget airline that only flies internally. No international flights. So, we are a regional budget airline with a domestic clientele that flies mostly for business. But now let us imagine we also offer other airline staff the opportunity to gain flying hours and practice flying planes. They get to co-pilot while they are still in training with bigger airlines that cover international markets. How does this change our market? How does this make us competitive? Would it harm our reputation if the public knew about our business model? If they knew that most of our flights were flown by the co-pilot who was still being trained. Do you think this might harm our market share?

Of course, it all depends on perceptions and how we position ourselves in the market. Perceptions of who we think we are and the perceptions that the public have of us may be two quite different things. The first thing any company or organization needs to do is to figure out exactly what market they are actually in. Once they know and understand this, they need to research their market.

Furthermore, you need to define what is meant by the terms used. Define the term *regional airline* and what it means to be a *premium airline*. Once we have a better grasp of this, we can start to do the heavy lifting of data capture and data analysis. As we start to look at the size of the markets for the various offers, we have identified regional versus national versus international, budget versus premium and so on. No matter which market we are in, there are always competitors of varying size and influence. Knowing how much each of these have in their market will give you a clear indication of the market share each competitor controls at the time of the analysis. That is because markets are always in flux. They change over time and can disappear entirely as new and emerging markets come to prominence. But the bottom line remains the same for all, the offer that the organization brings to market needs to be wanted by the customer. By being in demand at some level, market share is gained.

This is basic business knowledge, but the fact you know which market you are in can give you a clear advantage over those that are more hesitant, unsure, or plain wrong about the market they serve. The definitions produced to outline the market you are in can aid you even more by providing you with parameters for the huge amount of data you will gather on your market in the broadest sense. A parameter is important as it helps set limits to the research you do on the market. This helps you gain more focused insights. Instead of just looking at the games market, you can look at the games market for board games. Instead of all board games, you can start examining different genres of board games. This results in an ever-decreasing circle of what constitutes a competitor, your market, and the size of that market. Here we have the single most important aspect of the data you uncover – size. Naturally, the question to ask:

- Exactly how big is this market?

Now you can see why the definitions of the market and the parameters need to be so carefully considered. The more accurate the definitions of the market, the better you know what to measure. You will be confident addressing these questions:

- How many people buy-in that market?
- How much do they spend in transactions?
- When will this money get spent?
- How many companies operate in that market?
- How big are these companies?
- Where are these companies based?
- How long have they been operating?
- What aspects of the market do they serve?

All can be answered using secondary research methodologies. Online searches, library and local government databases, local community clusters, and even key opinion leaders (influencers) can hint at much of this information. Being smart in your approach to the desk research you do will yield better results. For example, using Bing, DuckDuckGo, Google will provide you with a much wider view of the internet than using just one of these search engines. They may even give you different perspectives of the market based on their different data sets they retrieve for you. None of which would have been visible if you had not conducted basic research into the make-up of your market. Knowing you can reach and sell to an adequate market share will be more likely to mean your project being economically sustainable over the longer term. It can also result in costs being reduced that can result in a distinct competitive advantage over rivals in that market.

If company 'A' can buy-in the services and resources it needs cheaper than company 'B', then the materials needed in the creation of the product being brought to market are obviously lower. That means that company 'A' can build or create what the market desires at a lower cost. If company 'A' and company 'B' sell at the same price, then company 'A' is more likely to have higher profits. Because it makes higher profits, it has more power and it may be able to dictate to the whole market certain conditions. Price is an obvious example.

As company 'A' has bigger profits and thus more money in the bank, it could use it to support lower prices of products that put pressure on some of its rivals. It can use this cash to focus on research and development (R&D), bringing ever more creative products to the market and it can start to dictate the price of labour in a market. By paying staff higher salaries or offering better benefits, it may start to adjust the benchmark in the market over things like pay and conditions for the people that work in that market. In this way, it can start to help company 'A' retain the best people and sustain its market share. The ability of company 'A' to gain the upper hand produces a ripple effect. Assuming their use of these additional profits are used to produce a strategic advantage, the shape of an entire market can start to be dictated by a company that has, for now, a bigger spend ability than the competitors.

This is a basic scenario; it papers over many problems and issues. But it serves us well to help understand why adequate market share is so important to the planning process. Knowing the scale and likely profitability of the project can help indicate the outcome of starting this venture. Of course, the main component here is the customer. We have not asked or interrogated any real people about their needs and desires. Much more importantly, we need to ask potential customers, not just people in general for their input on our project. In other words, we have not yet conducted any research using primary methodologies. So far, it is all second-hand information we are relying on. At this stage, we can relax a little as our concern is more with the market size rather than the customer's specific requirements. This is important; we will focus on that later in the planning process. Right now, our concern is with the competitors, the rivals and colleagues that are already on the market offering these customers value in some shape and form. One of the most effective tools to do this analysis is a STEEPLE analysis that should be followed by a better-informed SWOT analysis.

This is unconventional wisdom. Most management material will only include a SWOT analysis and tend to overlook the importance of the STEEPLE analytical tool for informing a SWOT. These are brilliantly simple tools for offering a novice enterprise project a healthy look at their markets and the possibilities that may exist there. STEEPLE stands for:

- Sociocultural
- Technological
- Economical
- Environmental
- Political
- Legal
- Educational

These seven areas are of concern for any market and should be analysed prior to conducting a SWOT analysis because they provide greater insight into the market conditions that your project will operate in. These insights can then be used to inform the SWOT analysis.

There are two ways to perform the analysis; one is to focus on the future scenarios that can be predicted based on the secondary research you have conducted. The other is to look at the external market conditions that exist right now and to think about how this impacts the project in the short to medium term. Either way, what you are trying to uncover is the impact these factors will have on the project's preliminary stages, the stages where the ideas are still being formulated and informed by this type of analysis. In either approach, the task at hand is to ask questions related to each of the sections.

These are all *external* factors that have an *internal* impact. In scenario one, where STEEPLE is used to look at future conditions in the market, the task is to ask what can be predicted based on the secondary research findings. For example, imagine you are building a game to help visitors of heritage sites understand the history. The section on sociocultural might state:

> based on the findings from our secondary research on heritage sites, we can predict that heritage sites are likely to increase their revenues because of a growing interest in our social development as a society. The demographic that visits these sites are 55+ and the general population is increasing in this demographic category.

We can use the data to tell us the impact this interest is having on the market right now. For example, 'according to the findings of [sight source] we can see that the market is presently in a growth phase which provides comfort that we are entering a stage where people are interested in this offer and the wider market for heritage sites.' Or, seen another way, 'people are presently spending record amounts in heritage markets as their income levels have increased and interest due to public awareness in heritage more broadly is gaining traction [sight source].'

Immediately, it has an impact on how we view the trade that is happening in that market. Insights gained can be provided for the reader of the plan based on sound empirical observations we have made about the trading conditions (see Section 8.1). This style of interrogation can now be repeated in all the sections of the STEEPLE. For example, questions which may get posed:

- Sociocultural: How is an ageing population affecting our sector of the games market?
- Technological: What are the consequences of innovative technologies on our game?
- Economical: Are there significant economic forecasts that may affect our ability to trade?
- Environmental: Can we foresee any regulatory or moral duties we should comply with?
- Political: What impact will a changing political environment have on our trading?

- Legal: Do we predict compliance or regulatory changes?
- Educational: Are there trends that may impact the way we communicate?

These are not meant to be high-level questions that require a PhD to answer. They are more about the near-future predictions which are being made based on your findings about the market and the conditions of trading in that market. Sometimes they can be deceptively simple. Take education as an example. We focus on the ability to communicate and educate your CUPs as opposed to the educational system found in any state. The question then shifts from one of the outputs of primary, secondary, or tertiary educational providers to one that focuses on impression management through advertising, marketing, and public relations. Education is focused on constructing a message that helps CUPs take informed action based on these activities.

Political questions are also deceptive. The level is missing in this question; are we to think about the local, national, or international changes? Are all three relevant? It is unlikely that the reader of your business plan will require an essay on the changes in the political landscape on a global scale. The most significant changes are the ones to include and these in turn must also be relevant to the game and the market you are entering.

All this can lead to better-informed SWOT analysis of the internal and external conditions. SWOT stands for strengths, weaknesses, opportunities, and threats. It is divided between the internal (strengths and weaknesses) and the external (opportunities and threats). Having completed the STEEPLE analysis, the reader of the business plan can gain a much deeper understanding of the market and your position in it.

A SWOT analysis is most useful when clear objectives for doing one are outlined; in other words, the purpose of the analysis is established and the use of the tool in being able to understand these objectives is clearly outlined. This can help in the analysis of the market and the competition that exists. The simplicity of both a STEEPLE and a SWOT should not detract from the powerful insights these tools can provide. There is always a bias present as choices are made on what elements get analysed in the headings. Again though, clear objectives can help balance this with more objective insights into the reality of the market conditions.

These tools are also there to provide guidance on the strategic choices for the project. By balancing strengths with opportunities, or strengths to threats, or weaknesses to threats, the real conditions in the market can be exposed. By doing so, a clearer strategic pathway may emerge as the conditions reveal themselves. But this also leads to decisions that need to be made on the strategy that will best serve the project. This is where the simplicity behind these tools can get complex.

5.4 Success

The need to identify key success factors will result in the plan approaching the market with a clear line of thought on the strategic choices being made. It will also help the games business think about who will be involved and where the talented folk that will help build the business and the game, will come from. In other words, team assembly can begin, and where the skills in the present team are found lacking so action can be taken to compensate. This could be in the form of hiring new talent to fill this gap or training existing folk in the project so they may take on these responsibilities.

By identifying these weaknesses, there is potential to address them and turn them into a strength. The greatest benefits of addressing the key success factors for an early-stage project is that the enterprise gets buy-in from the teams involved. Both internally and externally. That is because with clearly articulated key success factors, people can understand the direction of travel and make sense of the decisions management is making. Clearly articulated, codified key success factors provide a compass reference that everyone should be able to understand.

Beyond this they also help to benchmark where the project is against the strategic goals that have been set to help meet the mission of the project. For example, your game may be seeking a higher feedback score on comparison sites, higher sales, user diversity, or peer recognition as the quantifiable measurement to assess if the game is meeting its goals. Specific key success factors can be measured against these criteria and the overall level of activity can be appraised, this means a better understanding of where things are and where things are headed.

These are also important as part of the reflection on what has been achieved in the recent past. By looking back and taking stock of these achievements one can see concrete outcomes of our actions. This can help keep us motivated by focusing on what our achievements have been and acting as a driver for the future short to medium term. It is easy to lose track of how far we have come, especially when starting a fledgling project. There can be weeks, or even months, when the entire process just feels like a drain on our emotional well-being. Actions feel like they take us nowhere, while we are achieving things and making progress. Once again though, having clearly defined key success factors can act as a guide, a clear indication of what has been achieved, and how this adds to the overall vision. This can be a powerful motivator, helping us to see the progress and changes that have evolved. Key success factors provide a clear set of strategic accomplishments.

So, the key success factors cannot be ignored. They serve many functions and can even help us demonstrate to the wider stakeholders in the project what has been achieved, the logic of why key success factors have been chosen, and how you intend to reach these in the future. For the fledgling start-up this can prove more problematic than for an established project because all too often the start-up lacks confidence about what its strategic decisions will accomplish. For either the start-up or established project, the tendency is towards more conceptually solid key success factors that can be measured against performance over a given period. Formal accounting is one example, where savvy stakeholders will understand the patterns they see overtime. It should be remembered though, that this is only one set of measurements against the operational context of the project.

As we saw above, key success factors can come in many forms of quantifiable aspects of the project. Key success factors may, for example, be focused on player or customer acquisition, product development, employee satisfaction, organisational culture, achievement against mission, ability to pivot, or adoption of recent technology. This is by no means an exhaustive list. But it does serve to demonstrate how diverse key success factors can be and it also serves to demonstrate how these can be introduced to show milestones being achieved that are far beyond purely accounting or financial aspects of the project. Differentiating accounting and finance of the project is a necessary distinction to make and either can be used in formulating your key success factors.

But here we encounter another danger. The sheer volume of choices can be overwhelming. At some point, a choice needs to be made about which key success factors you are going to choose and a justification for their choice. This is going to be reliant on the market the project operates in. That is because some key success factors are a better fit with certain markets. It should also be remembered that they will need revision periodically.

This brings us to another issue which is the fact that they may be time sensitive. They may not be relevant in the longer term as the project starts to become established and grows. The key success factors may not be fixed, they may be great to act as a guide for the project in the preliminary stages, or when the project is being planned. But there should always be an accepted logic that these will change and shift over time. They should be allowed to evolve and as they do so as they will help inform the key performance indicators that will be used to measure organisational performance against expectations, strategically decided upon, and set by management. These are later management tools, and they serve a similar function as key success factors but differ in that they are more about the mission. In this respect, they act more like guiding principles against which success is more closely aligned with the success of the mission. The mission reflects the values and operational parameters by which the project will operate. Think of the key success factors being more about establishing links between the values in the culture of the project and the overriding strategic goals. Goals that are important to the success of the project.

Key success factors should not be used to indicate the health of a market externally to the project. They are there to help keep things on track, but they can be poor tools for demonstrating the health of a market. Whereas the key performance indicators may be able to indicate where there may be issues with the project's strategy and the market more broadly. Key success factors are not good indicators against these factors because, as should be clear by now, they are more for internal measurement. Although they may produce some indication of what's happening externally, they should not be relied on in isolation as an early warning system for market tendencies. This also serves to reinforce the point made earlier that these are not fixed but in a state of flux. The future performance and success of the project is probably reliant on the ability to react to changes and shifts in the market. The key success factors are poor at measuring or predicting these changes. It's beyond the scope of the key success factors to do so and these challenges are better quantified against the key performance indicators.

References

Cova, B., Kozinets, R.V. & Shanker, A. (2011), *Consumer Tribes*, Abingdon: Routledge.

Ranchhod, A. & Gurău, C. (2007), *Marketing Strategies: A Contemporary Approach*, Harlow: Pearson Education Limited.

6
BRANDING

What is your purpose?

A fundamental question that as you get into the business planning writing process, you must be able to answer. Games are competing head-to-head with each other in the market, from early-stage ideas found on crowdfunding platforms to online marketplaces where board games can be produced and sold (cf. gamecrafter.com). Creative project identity is needed to help the game stand out in these noisy and sometimes overcrowded marketplaces. This is the brand. It is the set of identifiers that make your game special in some way and often come to represent the emotional attachment that consumers feel when they recall your game.

A brand has been compared to things (products and services) having a personality that is unique and special. Just like your family, friends, colleagues, and neighbours. They all have individual ways of doing things and being in this world, and so it is for the brand that you create to portray the game. The things you stand for and the purpose of the project should somehow be embedded in the brand image that gets projected out to the world and received by your CUPs.

At the most basic level, brands are a way to differentiate things. They do this by using certain colours, images, typeface, and tone they use to communicate. There are dangers with all this and getting it right is often down to multiple attempts until something relevant emerges. The alternative is to hire an outsider to come in and create the branding for the game. But even then, there are lots of things to consider and of course this will come with a price tag attached. If you are bootstrapping the game, this may not be the best option. Perhaps, you don't even need to be thinking about branding the game at this stage?

When you listen to communication experts from marketing or public relations, they can be quite persuasive on their position that branding is essential for communication and engagement

 DOI: 10.1201/9781003352594-6

with a targeted audience, that this is what the public want, even demand, a kind of conversation with the brand and the consumer to know, understand, and even love that brand. But Dunsdon (2015) offers a critique that is quite persuasive. His position is that very few brands are willingly in conversation with their consumer tribes. The idea that two-way communication is an attractive one because this is what the customer wants is, in his view, erroneous. The brands, where this is perhaps most likely for Dunsdon, fall into one of three categories synthesised below:

- Brands that resonate with you because of a genuine shared passion.
- Brands that resonate with you because their purpose relates to a cause you believe.
- Brands with extreme paradigms that act as a bond for a community.

(Dunsdon, 2015: 184)

If you know the answer to the question what *is your purpose*, and your game doesn't fit any of the criteria above, then being brave enough to accept that people may not want to listen to you may in fact save you resources and enable you to discover where the permission for communication with your tribe exists. It may be that the first 100 customers want a personal touch and enjoy meeting you and providing you with feedback on the game. But that is not scalable for the project. What happens when you reach 5,000 customers or 50,000? The team won't have the bandwidth to satisfy all these people and assimilate their feedback into a coherent strategy, not at speed anyway.

Perhaps, a better approach would be to think about how you can be baked-in to the memory of the customer, not the players or users, the customer. For they make the decision to purchase. The CUPs of any game are suffering a drought in terms of time. Therefore, the game needs to be able to make associations in the mind of the customer that get triggered when they are making a purchasing decision. Bogusky and Winsor (2009) referred to marketing as necessarily being baked-in from the start of a product's life cycle. This is very similar. It means the customer must do less active thinking about the product; it's an almost automated response to the brand. Too much information has the effect of stumping our actions, a paralysis by analysis. If we accept Dunsdon's position, then actually brands should be trying to help customers not to think, which, in his view, is a better strategy.

- Is this too risky for you as you start out on your branding journey?
- Should you consider a strategy that involves you 'talking' to all your customer base?

These are hard choices with no absolute answer for your project. Whichever you choose, the main thing to remember is that the branding you develop is both internal and external. The internal connection with your culture, no matter how small or focused you are, this is the stuff you stand for. It incorporates and highlights the identity of the project. This is important as it helps to bring on board the kind of people you want on board and allows you to reach out and recruit as you grow with the potential to make this aspect visible, which in turn can act as a draw for more talent to join you. External branding connects the customers' perceptions of the project. This is about how people view you from outside. It connects your associations concerning your purpose and what you stand for. You have less control over these external emotional connections that the customer has with your brand, but it is important you consider this.

There is also the need for you to do things that you say you will do. Claiming you are environmentally leaning and then using toxic inks and producing goods that involve worker conditions that are harmful is going to unbalance the claims you are making. This will create cognitive dissonance [hover for explanation] in the minds of the CUPs. This in turn may create reputational damage. Something to avoid.

- But what if you cannot avoid it?
- How can you be a bad brand with a good reputation?

Reputation and brand are very closely aligned, and Amazon is a brand that has a bad reputation and a good brand. That's because the reputation is more about the things that have been done, while the concept of brand is more emotional from both internal and external views (Jones, 2017).

But coming back to Dunsdon's point above, the problem is that humans learn over time to trust others well. To want to be in conversation with these brands the more trust the CUPs will want to have with them. The problem is that this takes a long time to build. As you are starting out, building trust can only be done by delivering on the things that you promise. In an age where the idea of truth is complicated and the review of companies and their work is becoming more open and accessible by the customer, it is imperative that you remain as transparent and trustworthy as possible (de Chenecey, 2019).

6.1 Position

Related to this is the idea that the brand must take a position. What we mean by this is the difference between the personality and proposition which is aligned with the internal and external dimensions we discussed above. This works by viewing the brand as having a personality and that this gets portrayed somehow to the audience and means something to them on an individual level. The proposition, on the other hand, refers to the value the brand creates and the feelings this evoke in people when they think about the brand (Jones, 2017). This also helps bring us full circle to Dunsdon's unique take on brands making more of these associations and less about trying desperately to talk to their consumer base.

Position follows once the consumer segment (who you will target) and the strategy for targeting them have been established. For the plan it's a logical sequence, you know the who (as in who are your CUPs) and now you know the how (as in how you will do this and when). Then you need to follow this with the image the brand wants to convey in the CUPs mind. Again, there are complexities if the image sought is differentiated between the customer, user, or player. If this is the case in your plan, then you will need, in simple terms, to lay out for the reader why this strategy is optimal in your context and how this will be implemented. But remember to keep this simple, don't over complicate this aspect.

Choosing the targets in a game market is by many measures one of the more complex activities for you to make judgements about. It demands an understanding of the core market and the periphery that is connected to the core. Segmenting your market means thinking about the motivations of the CUPs (with emphasis normally on the customer). As an example, Newzoo (2019) created a set of eight personas of gamers that they use in their segmentation of video gamers while the International Games Developer Association (research syndicated with NPD) breaks the USA market into six segments based on behaviour (IGDA, 2019). There are numerous ways you can approach this, from monetisation in the game, level attainment or social buzz, the final decision needs to be explained in simple terms in the business plan. It may be that you decide to segment based on value (low price), mid-market (average price), or premium (high end price), with each one representing a target sales group that you are going to attract with the game.

Tied closely to this is the targeting strategy that you adopt in your marketing plans. This means you have three levels to think about:

- Undifferentiated marketing strategy.
- Differentiated marketing strategy.
- Concentrated marketing strategy.

Choices are available as to the different approaches you decide as optimal to communicate with your CUPs. This gets complex when we target CUPs differently, if we learn in our research that 'users' react better to a different message than we found optimal for the 'customer', then things get complex because we are tasked with creating far greater numbers of messages. This is a positive step; it means we have even greater cognition of these groups and their motivations. But of course, this creates more tasks as fresh messages are needed for the different segments.

An undifferentiated marketing strategy will see the project choose a strategy that will result in one set of messages being broadcast to the whole market. A kind of scattergun approach that means blasting all the channels with the same messages to all CUPs simultaneously. It's only targeted on the market holistically and there may be dangers that the message that gets pushed out might appeal to some segments and not others. Worse, it may even alienate some of the very segments we wanted to attract.

Differentiated is where the different strategies are aligned with different segments of the market. If your game is proposing to deliver different messages to customers, users, and players, then this is the strategy you consider optimal. It's complex because, as we saw, it means more work creating the messages and more work to measure the results of the different messages. However, the payoff is a more personalised set of messages that can be more appealing to the targeted segment.

A concentrated marketing strategy is a mix of the above. A single message is targeted to each of the segments. Where the undifferentiated strategy was broadcasting to the whole market, without segmenting it further, this strategy targets each segment with an optimal message. Again, it can be complex given the issues above, but once again this can be attractive as it is more aligned with the identified needs and motivations of the target group as shown in Figure 6.1.

Making this kind of choice leads to a position being adopted that means you have an outline, or idea, of how the brand will be received by the target CUPs (again, normally with a focus on the customer). It might be worth changing the term 'target' to 'meaning' or 'impression', and it now becomes imperative that this image impression is managed well. Traditionally, the brand will attempt to engage and interact with the targeted CUPs, but this is frequently questioned by experts in contemporary markets as it may in fact mean interruption rather than engagement. But as we saw above, engagement itself becomes problematic if it means unnecessary conversations and results in more disruption. More non-consensual attempts at interactions with the

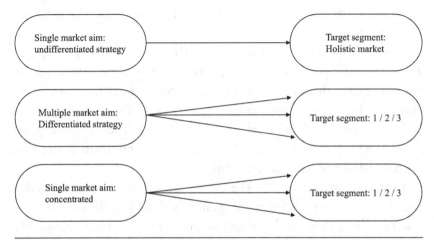

Figure 6.1   Three marketing mixes.

brands are stuck in the old dichotomy of trying to communicate to a group who don't desire this.

According to Jones (2015), the games industry might already have the answer. His critique of the industry leads him to the conclusion that using game techniques could offer brands an opportunity to do something new and innovative. Using game techniques could influence behavioural changes that are desired by the brands themselves, while also creating a better position in the minds of the consumer.

Jones (2015) thinks this is possible using game elements to produce behavioural changes among the targets. When we talk about marketing and the brand we wish to promote, 'interruption' has given way to 'engagement' and 'attitude' to 'action'. This is the new paradigm for creating brands. Jones (ibid) believes these elements are also in flux and to demonstrate how, he introduces the concept of play. In this context, play is not something that can be hoisted into branding or marketing but needs to be part of the combination that is baked-in. It then follows that all marketing, in whatever form, has an element of play embedded in it. This brings us full circle to Dunsdon (2015) and the concept of engagement to some form of relevance to our segments. It's an interesting concept that continues with the idea that branding and marketing are not fixed and are always in flux. Evidence can be provided in the very fact that brands are moving targets for the consumer and their position in any market is transient. A position is not fixed and getting our CUPs to play with our brands may yet prove to demonstrate how this element can add to the desired behavioural changes we may seek.

An easy way to think about this is to think about quality and price. From the example in Figure 6.2, you can see the two axes, quality running vertically and price horizontally. Now we can mark where we think the brands (we can also use this technique for products) should be positioned based on what we feel and experience. A perceptual map, like the one in Figure 6.2, is a good demonstration of the ease with which this can be demonstrated:

Let's start with Brand C. We can see that it has a high price compared to the others and that the quality is also high. This might be a good position; they are charging a premium price for premium quality (at least in the mind of the consumer).

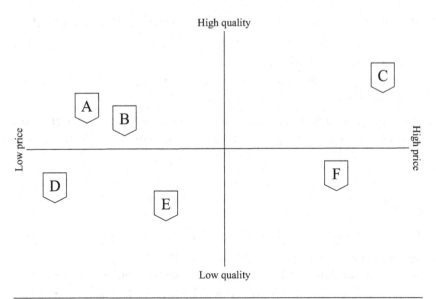

Figure 6.2 Perceptual mapping example.

Compare this with Brand F. They have a problem; they think they are a premium product/brand, but the quality is low. This results in the consumer not purchasing because Brand C is perceived as better value for money. Almost the same price, but better value.

Brand A is a bigger problem for both Brand C and Brand F. Brand A has a low price and is also perceived as high quality. In this scenario, they are the problem for both brands C and F to compete with as they seem to be doing well on both factors.

Brand B is also good quality but not perceived as good as Brand A, even though Brand B comes with a little lower price tag, they may be in a better position over the longer term than Brand A if their margins are higher.

Brand D is the value brand of the group. Low price but this comes with accepted low quality.

Brand E on the other hand is similar, but they are in perhaps the most dangerous position. Their quality is the lowest of all the brands. The danger is that they lose sales because of this and then find they are struggling to raise enough money to improve the quality.

The issue then becomes about margins. Brand A looks good, but to keep that quality level might mean they are not making as much profit as Brand C. Even though brand A is selling more, they might not be able to bank as much of that money as Brand C. This could be dangerous in the longer term as market shocks can squeeze the smaller profits Brand A is making.

This mapping technique can be used on almost any two factors. You just need to change the axis heading and determine where the features are in relation to each other. It's simple and most effective when used to support the points and arguments being made in the business plan.

6.2 IP

Intellectual property (IP) is the term for the protection you can give to your creative output. It was originally designed to offer you a window of opportunity to build a business around your creative outputs by protecting you from being copied by others. In effect, it means a temporary monopoly for you and the project through commercialisation or with others that could use your creative output to these ends.

There are several types of IP, which we cover in this chapter, and they are all quite different in the levels of protection they offer. It's also possible to allow others to have access to your creative innovation while generating some revenue from it (licensing it for others to use) or alternatively you can allow others to build on your innovation and share their contribution with others, using a creative commons licence. There are also options to register some types of IP while others are assigned automatically. *Automatically assigned* means you can tell others you are claiming the IP without the need to pay or register anywhere. An example is this book, it is licensed with a copyright symbol, the C in a circle: ©. This tells people that the work (the creative output) is owned by someone, and this means that the original creator must be acknowledged if bits are used in other work or licensed if others want to use the whole text for their own purposes. The name of the copyright owner should always follow the © symbol and this is followed by the year. No IP is infinite, protection always expires at some point, and therefore the year is important. It's also possible for more than one person, or entity, to own IP protection.

For example, imagine someone has the brilliant idea (?) of creating a musical based on Business Planning for Games. This person cannot just copy the text and create the musical. They will need to contact the publisher and get permission to use the content of the book, even if they create derivatives of this original work. Once this is agreed, which normally involves a financial deal, the theatre producers can get to work and start creating their own creative output, The Business Planning for Games Musical.

The point is the original book (or game or whatever) can have protection granted by the state jurisdiction. This is where IP really helps and even with the use of creative commons licences (see below), the creator still has protection, but they are allowing others permission to use the work under certain circumstances in certain restricted ways. But it does allow a more dynamic approach to the work. Table 6.1 outlines whether the rights are automatic, the terms, and where to find out more.

Copyright is by far the simplest protection you can gain. It covers the following outputs:

- Artistic, dramatic, film, literature, or musical outputs, all covered for the creator's lifetime plus 70 years after their death. In an instance where there is more than one creator, the 70-year deadline starts from the date of death of the last author. If work is published posthumously, it is covered for 50 years.
- Scores for games, directorships, dialogues, screen plays, and television and radio outputs are covered for 50 years from their first broadcast.
- Typographical layouts are covered for 25 years from the date of creation.

Design rights can be claimed without registration, but stronger protection can be granted if these designs meet the eligibility rules. Things like contours, shapes, and materials can be registered. They are registered for five years at a time and can be repeated for up to 25 years. Designs can also be registered for up to one year after they are first made public.

Domain names are registered with a domain provider (cf. Domain. com, GoDaddy.com or One.com). These can be renewed annually or longer. It's always worth taking some time to consider the domain name you use. It should fit the game and ideally link the purpose of the project through the name.

Table 6.1   IP Terms and Help

IP NAME	AUTOMATIC	TERM	HELP
Copyright	Yes	Varied depending on the output.	https://www.gov.uk/topic/intellectual-property/copyright
Design Rights	Yes (unregistered) No (registered)	25 years maximum.	https://www.bl.uk/business-and-ip-centre/articles/what-is-my-automatic-design-right
Domain names	No	Depending on the terms of the provider (can be renewed annually with most providers).	https://www.gov.uk/guidance/keeping-your-domain-name-secure
Patents	No	20 years.	https://www.gov.uk/topic/intellectual-property/patents
Trademarks/ Logos	™ Yes (unregistered) ® No (registered)	™ unlimited. ® 10-year cycles.	https://www.gov.uk/topic/intellectual-property/trade-marks

Patents are the most expensive and the most time-consuming type of IP protection you can gain. They are also not the golden ticket to market monopoly that some people think they are. As with any IP, you may need to fight to stop others infringing your rights and this will often mean court proceedings, or at the very least the involvement of specialists to help defend your rights. This is going to be expensive and time consuming. There are also significant differences in the protection patents grant you in other states. A UK patent, for example, means very little in Russia where the 2022 decree 299 of the civil code means that patents granted in unfriendly countries are not valid in the state (The Economist, 2022). If you decide to patent your game, it will need to be eligible against a strict set of conditions of which we do not have the space to detail here, Table 6.1 provides a link to the UK IP Office (IPO) where more up-to-date and relevant information about the process can be found.

Trademarks and logos are easier for you to claim in the business plan. That's because the public can see these forms and they help inform the position the game will command in the mind of your CUPs. There are two types of trademarks, these are either assigned automatically (where you see ™ at the end of the name or logo) or they can be registered for a small fee with the IPO (where you see ®). These forms of IP can be names, typefaces, and graphical representations. There are restrictions and you are encouraged to see the IPO link below to find the latest requirements for the granting of a trademark, especially for game producers as there are strict rules over the use of certain terminology, images, and in the way things can be configured. This can be problematic for games as the use of crests or nationalist symbols are often not allowed.

It must be remembered that IP can be challenged, and this can be an expensive and drawn-out process. Even if you were to win in court, the reputational damage disputes may be long lasting for a nascent game producer. Help should be sought if you are thinking of patenting your invention for the game and even with simple forms of IP, think about the best way to protect your ideas against the likelihood of them being used by others without your permission. Likewise, always do thorough checks to make sure you have not infringed anyone else's IP in the process of making your game. Always keep a proper record of any searches you have conducted.

This is a much more fluid task today with the kind of databases we have in the UK with the IPO, they can help you search and gain basic insights into names, logos, and even patents. For copyrighted material, the British Library is the best place to search. IP is not something to fear; it is there as a way to protect you and is more about using common sense when considering the levels of protection you think you will need for your game.

It may be that the work you want to use is still in copyright, but you cannot trace the original creator or the publisher. This is called ghost copyright. You may use this material, but you should keep tight records of the investigative work you have done to find both the original creator and the publisher in order to seek permission to use this work. Be prepared to be challenged if you do use ghost copyright work.

Creative Commons are a relatively new way to licence copyrighted materials (see creativecommons.org). The exact configuration of the licence is open for you to construct as best fits the work you have produced and what you want to allow others to do with the original work, including sharing it with others. Creative commons do not mean you give away your copyright output, it means you allow others to automatically do things with the original output that would otherwise have been restricted. For example, you might want others to be able to add to your original work and share it under the same licence as you have offered, but with the restriction that these others cannot make money from the derivative of the work they produce. This is all possible under creative commons. If this does interest you, then it is worth exploring the different licence constructs possible via the link provided above.

References

Bogusky, A. and Winsor, J. (2009), *Baked In: Creating Products and Businesses That Market Themselves*, Chicago: B2 Books.

de Chenecey, S.P. (2019), *The Post-truth Business: How to Rebuild Brand Authenticity in a Distrusting World*, London: Kogan Page.

Dunsdon, A. (2015), I Believe in the Age of Osmosis, In Nick Kendall (ed), *What Is A 21st Century Brand: New Thinking from the Next Generation of Agency Leaders*, London: Kogan Page, pp. 179–195.

IGDA (2019), *Gamer Segmentation Report*, Toronto: IGDA, https://igda.org/resources-archive/2018-2019-gamer-segmentation-report-white-paper/

Jones, R. (2017), *Branding: A Very Short Introduction*, Oxford: Oxford University Press.

Jones, T. (2015), I Believe in Gaming Your Brand, In Nick Kendall (ed), *What Is A 21st Century Brand: New Thinking from the Next Generation of Agency Leaders*, London: Kogan Page, pp. 65–82.

Newzoo (2019), *Newzoo's Gamer Segmentation™*, Amsterdam: Newzoo, https://newzoo.com/news/introducing-newzoos-gamer-segmentation-the-key-to-understanding-quantifying-and-reaching-game-enthusiasts-across-the-world

The Economist (2022), *Has Russia Legalised Intellectual-Property Theft?*, 04.06.2022, pp. 58–59.

7

MARKETING

Marketing is all about markets and how to communicate among the chaos and abundance of the voices that will already be vying for attention. For you and your game, it's about communicating with an identified set of people about the game and the benefits that it will have for them, their friends, and their family. Communicating about the brand can be problematic as this is not yet established. The game comes first. Once you have a place in your market and you have something of a following in those consumers who are buying your game, then the focus of your communication efforts can move to the branding of the organisation behind the game. Steps need to be taken to slowly build the momentum in CUPs understanding of the game and the vision being created via the project. If this happens too fast, it may be an indication that this is a fad, a short burst of interest that cannot be sustained.

Markets need to be understood on several levels from pure numbers of competitors to the motivation of the CUPs. Knowledge helps shape the type of communication you are going to use with your audience and the research you do is vital in helping you understand how these elements work in harmony (or otherwise). But the research, it must be remembered, has flaws. The results are interpreted by you and team members. All members will have a particular paradigm, and this will mean you segmenting a market or dividing up the competition in ways that make sense to you. The problem is that this may not make sense to the market.

This section in the business plan needs to demonstrate that you have a good understanding of the motivation of the CUPs and that your efforts of persuasion to get them to buy into your vision will be sufficient, that you can access the CUPs with implicit permission being granted to talk with these agents, via the channels you know

DOI: 10.1201/9781003352594-7

are optimal, and that the frequency with which you will use these channels to communicate is enough to produce engagement that will surpass expectations.

Right now, this may seem a daunting exercise because in effect you are being asked to develop a marketing strategy. But to have a strategy you need to know what the specific objectives of the project are. We have covered the general aims and objectives in Section 1.3, and these are now in need of alignment with the marketing plans you propose. In other words, the strategic marketing plan needs to follow the generic aims and objectives in making the game relevant to the targeted CUPs. When we recall Dunsdon's (2015) more radical position on this, suggesting you don't try to enter conversations but rather be relevant in some way to the CUPs, understanding the motivation of these agents helps us make sense of the exchanges they may find helpful, beyond a conversation about how good your game is and how it benefits them, the marketing strategy needs to think more about the relevance of the game to the lives of the CUPs.

This is a difficult thing to consider, and the text in the plan may need to work hard to convince the reader of the business plan as this is a newer approach than they may be used to. Perhaps a forked approach might be better for your game? This strategy is where you utilise traditional conversation pieces and then also try something more radical, perhaps on a different channel (see below), that helps demonstrate your relevance of the game to the tribe's lived experiences. If one strategy works better than the other, then you have some empirical evidence of what worked. It helps build your confidence and makes things more concrete for any future strategy.

7.1 Channels

Think about the organisations you interact with online. Brands you follow on LinkedIn and companies you track on Twitter are all granted permission to converse with you online because you have voluntarily decided to interact and allow the cultivation of support to be granted. Support here is in the most absolute basic terms of sheer numbers of interactions, not the more telling number of real people versus bots or levels of quality interactions these associates (algorithm or human) generate for these brands or products.

Support in these circumstances is implicit. You agree to terms and conditions that you have probably not read and probably not given much thought as you connect with the organisations you wish to follow. This is the permission that you must now seek. Permission to communicate with these people on some level. But it can be all too easy to be lazy in your approach and just throw out bland, uninspiring statements in the vague hope that some of your tribe pick-up on the chatter and start to natter.

This is way less likely to happen in reality. It will take time to build trust with the agents in your tribes. Even when you are focused on hot or political issues like ESG (environmental, social, and governance) issues, it is unlikely that tribes will converse with you straight away. An awkward social silence may follow. Friends and family can help, they can at least start to follow you and make some chatter on the channels of your choice.

Channels are important because they can trend, swinging in and out. Segments are found in general patterns on specific channels and it's important to be aware of new emerging channels that might be appropriate for your tribes to use or migrate too. But your task is to be able to pinpoint the channels you consider to be optimal for your game right now, as you start out on the marketing route.

This must be coupled with the aims and objectives of the project, where are you going, when will you get there, and how are all important questions to bear in mind as you start to plan your strategy for marketing. It may be that as you enter the channels with your shiny new game, you want to differentiate marketing messages for different tribes on different channels. This has been done in the past, it means more work for you as you must craft disparate messages that tie together for the tribes. Some being conversational pieces, while others are more a form of educational 'how to' type pieces of communication. But they serve the same objective in that they open the possibility for the tribes to be activated with your game.

7.2 Frequency

We can see from the above sections that marketing communication needs to be focused on the benefits the game produces with an emphasis at the start on the game, as opposed to the organisation behind the game. The planning you do in this regard also has to consider the frequency you will send out the messages you think will act to notify CUPs about the presence and benefits of the game. These need to be considered in terms of the quality of the messages that are being pushed out from you. If you are lucky, you will also be honoured with a pull, that is the reception of a message, or a like, or a retweet, that means your CUPs are into what you are doing. The danger of course is that these are negative pulls, in which case, swift action will be needed to counter these and make your case for the positives in the game.

When we consider the frequency, it might be helpful to think of the times in the day when your friends and family are most active on social media.

- Is their activity the same across all social media platforms?
- Or do they alter and modulate their frequency of use across the varied socials they use?

Going beyond friends and family:

- How about the identified CUPs?
- Taking the idea of learning about their patterns of use, can you then identify the patterns of use that your CUPs form in terms of their socials?

This is ultimately about rational strategic choices that you are going to use to maximise the exposure for the game to the CUPs segments that your research is indicating as the most likely to buy into the game. The pulse, or frequency, of message push should be easy to calculate by simply looking at the available analytics social media platforms themselves publish and third-party insights. Combining these should help you determine the pattern of social media signals that you push out to the audiences. But be aware, if these also create pulls which require time-sensitive responses, be prepared to work unsocial hours.

7.3 Marketing Prep

Sometimes it is easier to think in terms of chasing customers, acquiring new ones at frequent and regular intervals for the game. Expanding sales means more customers, right? It means being more economically sustainable because we have a fresh bunch of customers buying into our game every day, month, quarter, or year. This is surely a good place to be?

It is, yes. But what if you could turn these same customers into not just once and done purchasers of the game, but customers who buy additional value post that initial purchase. They transform into a customer who regularly buys more from you months after their initial decision and action to buy your game. Now that adds value. No longer are you just chasing the customer, to some degree, they are chasing you. Whether through:

- Subscriptions to premium services.
- Upgrades, or
- In-game purchases (see loot boxes in Section 4.1).

This ongoing revenue generating activity, where the customer has a longer-term relationship with the game, is frequently termed the *lifetime value* of the customer. Lifetime here is centred on the customer's relationship with the game and the project rather than the life expectancy of that customer. The customer enjoys their interactions and are willing to make further purchases over the duration of their time returning to play the game. This is finite and knowing when the end of this relationship is likely to be will help you determine when a new round of customer acquisition must be sought to replace the expiring one. When the game is new, that's no easy task. But spending some time to work this out can help justify the budget spend and constraints that you face.

Thinking this way is more entrepreneurial; it means not committing to continuously finding new customers but rather adding additional value for those you serve. Knowing who these customers are and their lifetime value means being able to produce more relevant KPIs (Key Performance Indicators) while also better understanding the revenues that can be gained. The result? A better understanding of the cash available to use on activities that will promote the game keeping existing customers engaged and attracting new customers at predicted intervals.

The key to this, when pulling together a marketing strategy, is to keep considering the game. It needs to be summarised in as brief a format as possible. Start with 50 words – no more. Outline what the game is about and bring in the benefits for the person making the purchase – the customer. Now repeat, if possible, for the user and the player. It may be there are only customers and players, in which case writing the 50 words just got more focused. It might help to list the functions of the game first and then list the benefits against these. Once you have these then start to craft the 50-word statement.

With the knowledge you have gained in writing the 50-word brief description and the budgets available, you can start to think about the offer to the early customers. The first few that will pay to have this game in their lives.

- What is it that you offer these people?
- Is there more than one type of benefit offered?

Answering these questions will create the communication insights that can lead to better quality messages being produced and distributed.

To answer the above questions, it may help to think about how the game is new and adds to the existing experience for each of the CUPs. For example:

- Is this game better than previous iterations of the genre?
- Does it reintroduce something from the past that has been overlooked or not used for some time?
- Is this game available in other formats?
- Can people get it from different outlets?
- What action are people encouraged to take next?

All these questions can add to the quality of the message being sent out to the CUPs. This can now be shown in the business plan, reinforcing for the reader confidence that the author of the plan is in control and knows what they are doing.

As well as novel action, there will also be a need for reaction. That is a response to the call to action in the message pushed out to the CUPs. In its simplest form, this will be to deal with negative comments and trolls on social media. But it also means an awareness of the Key Performance Indicators (KPIs) that will be used to track the impact of the communication. KPIs are created for the project to help management better understand the progress being made via the marketing plan. For example, let's imagine our game is for pure entertainment and is called 'Moodo'. We know players who have previously played Ludo (or variations of this game) will be attracted to Moodo. One of our KPIs, in this case, will be to raise awareness of Moodo among the Ludo playing community. Our marketing plan therefore will have a specific focus to attract these players.

- How will you know if you are being successful?

Simple analytics could help, tracing the number of visitors to the Moodo web store and how many convert from visitor to purchaser. If visitor numbers are high but sales are low, then something is obviously not working so well. There needs to be an adjustment to the plan. But at least you will be aware of this need and able to make necessary changes in the plan.

For the business plan, this will demonstrate your awareness of what the KPIs are and how they will help deliver a return on the marketing investment you decide to make. This return is where more is gained than the original expenditure, this is called a *Return on Investment* (abbreviated to RoI). This is strongly correlated with the channels and the content being pushed out to the target players of Ludo (in the context of the above example). That is the quality of the signal being sent is dependent on the persona being targeted and the correct, and timely, message being delivered to these personas through the appropriate channel. It might help to use a simple matrix, like the example shown in Table 7.1, to work out these elements of the marketing strategy.

This will make the connections with the persona, channel, content, and KPI much more instant and accessible. It clearly articulates the type of message on each channel and who they are targeted at. What is more, for the reader of the business plan, the KPI is aligned with

Table 7.1 Channel KPI Schedule

	PERSONA 1	PERSONA 2	PERSONA 3	PERSONA 4	
Channel	Tik-Tok	Twitter	Google Ads	Newsletter	Continue with each row adding data as required for your game.
Content	How to play & benefits of play.	1. Intro.2. How to play Moodo	Run ads for the game.	Moodo intro. & benefits of play.	
KPI	# Of views & shares	# Of comments & interactions	# Of sales via all outlets	# Of visitors to site + sales from visits	

these elements providing coherence for the whole strategy. Perhaps even more valuable for the team implementing this strategy is that it can also outline the parameters of the strategy. It clearly states the kind of content that will be used and by doing so, implicitly demonstrates the content that will not be used. It may even be worth explicitly stating this in the marketing plan or by adding a further row to Table 7.1, outlining what will not be used as part of the content or the channels that will be specifically excluded from the strategy. There could be any number of reasons for exclusion, one of the more obvious are reasons that contradict your own values or the mission of the project/organisational culture.

Reference

Dunsdon, A. (2015), I Believe in the Age of Osmosis, In Nick Kendall (ed), *What Is A 21st Century Brand: New Thinking from the Next Generation of Agency Leaders*, London: Kogan Page, pp. 179–195.

8
FINANCES

Now we turn to the financial aspirations you have for the project and an especially important question:

- How much money do you need to *survive* each month? Not the project, you personally?

Now try to answer this question:

- What are the aims of the project *in financial terms*?

For some in the games sector that may seem a hard set of questions to start the business plan. But think about this for a moment. If we do not know what kind of income we need to survive and what the actual financial aims of the business are, then

- How will we be able to tell if the project will keep us financially afloat?
- Or even if this project is going to be financially sustainable?

Now consider your KPIs.

- If you do not know how much money you burn through each month, how are you going to know if things are financially on track or not?

There is also a difference between accounting and finance that needs to be stated. In this section, we are concerned with the financing of the project, rather than the accounting of the movement of money in the project once we start trading. Finance is accepted (there are some arguments among experts) as the source of money that will help start and then grow the business.

Firstly, this section needs to outline your financial goals for the project. These need to be based on real-world research that has brought you to an understanding of the size of the market and how/why your project will not only survive in this market but thrive as an economically sustainable project, with a potential for growth.

When we talk about financial aspirations, there is always a danger that we want to talk about the financing of the project or the accounting equations that lead us to a declaration of profit or loss. That is quite different to what is expected in this section. Here, we are trying to outline the research we have done and what exactly this is telling us about the likelihood of the project meeting financial goals. Remember, it is you and your team that set the goals. They are created by you in the planning phases and so they should be achievable within the time frames that the team has set. That is important to remember: the simple idea that you have created the timelines within which things will be done.

Sometimes the metaphor of a runway is used to describe how much time, in financial terms, the project has left. The runway is calculated by how much money the project has in the bank divided by the amount the project is spending each month. So, let us say your project has £30,000 in the bank, but is spending £5,000 each month, then the runway is six months. In six months, the project will be out of cash. Therefore, the project needs to have lifted free of the runway in six months' time or it will still have contact with the asphalt and your take-off will need aborting.

Obviously, things could change; an investor may give you more money which means the runway gets extended, a grant might be accessed, or some product you have created gets sold and generates a boost to the finances, which again means the runway gets longer. Another option is to look at how costs could be reduced.

- How could the monthly spend rate be reduced enough to help extend the runway?

The danger of course is that an already tight situation (both in terms of resources and finances) gets even tighter. This may even lead to morale being lost among your team.

Monthly expenditures must be calculated based on your research findings. Within the financial aspirations we not only include where we want to be in some future period (three years, six years, etc.) but also what we predict to be the levels of monthly outgoing expenditure. What are we spending, on what exactly, and what value this expenditure creates. The emphasis is not on personal financial aspirations but those of the project. Essential to this aspect is the ability to calculate the sales and match these to the money that has been spent in developing the project. This calculation is known as the break-even.

The break-even calculation is one that will help the financial aspirations as it will not only show how much you need to sell to start making a profit but it will also show the units you will need to shift to get to the break-even point. First though, you need to have worked out all the costs involved in producing the game. That is everything money has been spent on, both fixed and variable costs. The difference between these lies in how the costs change when you produce more products. Some costs will be fixed, that is they do not change even when you make more of your product. For example, take a piece of software that gets purchased for £10. That software can be used to make one thing or 100 things. But the cost of the software remains the same.

Now imagine you need 100 units of electricity to make your product. If you make one product you use 100 units. If you make 10 products, then you will use 1000 units of electricity; the number of units used varies depending on the levels of production. Obviously, each unit costs money and so this becomes a variable (not fixed) cost to the project. Calculating and understanding all these different costs on something as complex as developing a game takes time and means that focus is needed to ensure everything is accounted for. Once this is done, then the break-even can be calculated by taking the costs together and looking at how many sales will be needed to match, and even better, get higher than that break-even figure.

Whatever the data is based on that leads to the analysis of the break-even, or any other financial assessment, it needs to be based on solid facts and data that have been obtained from the research that has been conducted. The financial goals must be realistic, they must be achievable, and they must be based on the data you have uncovered. That is why in this section it might be a good idea to be explicit about the databases and the secondary/primary research you have conducted to arrive at the timelines and financial goals you have set. Doing so will help build confidence into the plan and help the reader see how the financial goal fits into the plan for the project.

If the financial aspirations are too wild, they will either need taming or they will need justifying. Being ambitious for the project is a good thing, but the ambition you show must be realistic and doable. These aspirations need quantifying, how you do this depends on your game and the goals set. Try to answer this question:

- How do you quantify the aspirations you have for the project?

Quantitative research is needed. This research needs to demonstrate the accounting that has been put forward to show to the reader that this is a viable project. A project that can show a reasonable return on any investment and stability in the market you are entering with the potential for growth. But of course, this is the doctrine of business, and it may be that in your service to a specific community of practice that these principles are secondary at best. We can sense this is not going to be a simple exercise.

Neither is it going to be one that can be thrown together to add some window dressing to the plan. We should bear in mind some basic accounting rules; that the profit and loss statement cover the outcome of a period of trade. It represents how well a project did over that period (normally one year). It should be obvious that the start of this section needs both the *accounting* and the *financing* of the project to be articulated with clarity.

- But what about when you have no trading period?
- What happens when you are starting out, with nothing to show?

In Chapter 7, we thought about what the financial aspirations are for the project. In this section, we need to show the working outs of these aspirations. These are projections and so the reader understands that this is the equivalent of gazing into a crystal ball or swirling some loose tea leaves around in a near-empty cup to arrive at some statement of truth about the future. The key question to help kickstart this section is:

- How did we arrive at the assumptions we arrived at?

This is important because we need to be able to show that the projections we are making are based on real numbers and show that the financial aspirations are achievable within a specific timescale. The reality, of course, as stated above is that these are speculations you are making about the market. Any reader should be aware that the financial aspirations of the project are only based on assumptions being made about the market and your ability to convince that market to buy your product. This obviously changes once you have some trading completed that can be used to demonstrate levels of activity. But at the start, you do not have this privilege and so speculation, based on sound evidence and insights, is the only way to go.

This could be linked to your competitive advantage (see Section 1.7), where the advantage you have perceived as important for the market may well also be an insight for your financial aspirations. For example, let's imagine that the game you produce has unique features that, in play tests, are consistently reported as being the single most important thing in the game. These elements make it a 'must play' for your target segment. Your financial aspirations are to make £120 per day from the project. This means a healthy margin for the project and that you will be able to make drawings sufficient to cover your personal survival budget (for sole traders, drawings are money taken out of the business for personal use).

You have done the calculations; you know how many units are needed to sell each month to produce the £120 per day. Everything has been factored in, the cost of production, taxes, marketing, distribution, etc. This is also aligned with the overall strategy for the project. If this is convincing enough, you have the quantification for the section. It is not that complicated, but it does require early thought and planning. The strategy that has been developed, and outlined in full in the business plan, must be something that will be sustainable over the longer term. This means that the financial aspirations must include two stages: the starting out stage and the early next stage.

As the name suggests, the starting out stage is the exceedingly early stage where most important decisions are going to be made. That is because you still have the option to do nothing. To simply not start the project and not take any risks on the project. The early next stage is also important and carries a multitude of risks. That is because this stage is about where you go next, the decision is to stay as you are with limited potential for any further expansion or to grow the project into something bigger. Both stages carry risks (see Section 2.4), but both should also be based on the strategy that has been developed for the project. In the quantification of the financial aspirations for the project, a clear issue emerges for the reader.

- Will the competitive advantage be enough for our project to maintain sufficient income for us to meet our strategy?
- How will competition react to this offer?
- How will we generate sufficient sales of our game given the above insights?

The good news for you in the games sector, is your game! For you have a specific set of intellectual properties (IP) that can generate income. This makes it harder for competition to try and take market share from you. One way that might help in this area is to think of efficiencies in terms of your use of the IP.

- How much IP capacity do you have? [hover for link to explanation]
- How much could you have?
- What is the value of this IP?

By starting to think about your IP as something that adds value in economic terms to your project, you can start to quantify the value of these things. From the reader's perspective, this adds tremendous value and means that you, and the team, are getting to see the more concrete aspects of what you have created and the benefits this creative output can have for the project. In a way, it means intangible things are making the project more tangible.

8.1 Trade

Trade is essential to being able to survive. This is economic sustainability, the other side to the sustainability conversations we should be having. The basic premise is that products are created and/or acquired for something else to get assembled. This then gets sold for a higher price than it cost to create. A profit is made, which enables the process to start over again, creating more assembled things and, of course, more profit.

That is the basic principle, and it is easy to understand because in most capitalist states we are taught this basic scenario. There is a lot that is missing which helps define the brand or the CUPs or the purpose of the trading you are about to start. But these missing parts are less important in the business plan for the small start-up than they are for a major brand moving into a new geography or launching a radical new product. Trade for you is much simpler to understand and should be a reflection more of the levels of activities you are predicting based on your analysis of the research you conducted in Section 5.

But this section will ask you to make some speculation about the near future in terms of how things are predicted to be in the trading environment. Trade therefore reflects on the insights gained in Section 1.4, coupled with the insights from Chapter 5. This is sometimes difficult because there are some major world events that will affect your ability to trade and then there are hyper-local matters that will also have an impact. It is worth thinking of this section of the business plan like layers of an onion that consists of three layers: the macro, the meso, and the micro.

The outer layer, the largest as it covers the entire onion, is the macro layer and the best tool for understanding this layer is the STEEPLE analysis we were introduced to in Section 5.3. Understanding and answering these questions will help you portray a greater sense of the trading conditions you are dealing in and the impact this may have on this new venture. As we saw in Section 5.3, these questions are not designed to be super tricky to answer and should reflect the reality as you predict it. Some headings in the STEEPLE analysis will be less important to you, while others will be more relevant in the context of your game. Do not be afraid to provide more of an appraisal on certain questions over others, that is natural. Weighing the responses in this way will also make the business plan more convincing as the plan is written in a more tailored manner.

The middle layer, the meso layer, is the level of the games sector. This is a massive sector and includes many variable-sized firms that all contribute to the sector. This requires a SWOT analysis to help define the primary conditions of trading at this level. The key to SWOT is to divide the internal (strengths and weaknesses) and the external (opportunities and threats) to help build a more insightful and robust view of the competencies and resources your project has versus those found in the market.

Lastly, the micro layer is at the centre of the onion. These are the CUPs that have an interest in your game. They are the agents (the individuals) that sometimes form communities around the trading of the game or even game components but are more likely to be tribal in their organic attraction to certain genres of games. The micro level of your trade reflects the trends that are predicted in the genre of games for your project. Trend reports and creative (advertising) agencies can offer some insights at this level, but these tend to be focused on the global conditions of the trade in these genres. Nevertheless, these can be helpful in providing some evidence for the predicted state of trade in the near-to-middle term future.

These layers help you consider the conditions for trade, you now need to think about the scope of the trading, how big is the market and what is the range of the operational competition that is already embedded in the market?

Answers to these kinds of questions should have already been provided as you investigate your market and seek to understand the competition that will potentially impact your ability to trade. Understanding competitive competencies will add greater levels of knowledge capital for the team and help bolster the business plan.

8.2 Funding

What do you need funding for?

If your answer is to 'start the project', then this business plan will most likely fail to gain the kinds of reactions, you may have been hoping for. To start a project is a vague and ephemeral statement that does not allow anyone to buy into what you really want to achieve. Funding needs must be expressed as concise and focused statements. The reader must understand the needs that any funding fulfils. For commercial projects, the question *what do you need funding for?* could be turned around by the reader of the plan who may ask you, 'how do you go from zero to lots of sales?'

It is a reasonable question. If you are seeking funds, this often comes at a cost and may be seen as a way for you to mitigate personal risks (you are risking someone else's money, not your own), being able to answer this question concisely is going to add value to your plan. One option is bootstrapping, which could offer a solution.

Bootstrapping is a method of getting out there with the game and testing to see if the market reacts positively to the offer you are making. Its considerable risk as it means the founders of the game putting their own cash behind the prototype to see how CUPs react. These prototype products are labelled minimum viable products (MVPs), which gets translated in the games sector to minimum viable game (MVG). The MVG phase is in many ways the most important because here we are starting to gauge the reactions of the CUPs to the base idea of the game. Some elements of the game will be left out of these tests and some new elements will emerge as the game gets played and new insights are provided. For funding paradigms, this is important as the focus is on the use of the cash you need to help develop the game. Even when bootstrapping the project, the need to focus finances on the most important aspects of getting the MVG to test stages is essential. Just throwing money at the project will not make for compelling reading in this section. It needs to be thought through and stated in terms that will lead to something being possible – something that may yet emerge from the MVG.

Games will rarely be cash positive for the first few months. Sales take time to generate and the money that does materialise in a bank account may lag the point of sale. Cash flow needs careful consideration in these circumstances (see Section 8.4).

Stages of funding prescribe to the following:

- Grants/Awards (institutional or private)
- Pre-seed (founders, family, and friends)
- Seed (including crowdfunding)
- Series (A, B, C – from Business Angels or Venture Capitalists)
- IPO (Initial Public Offering)

Below is a list of 11 ways that your nascent project could be funded, with some insight on why this type of funding can help. This is not meant as a definitive list, and new and innovative methods of funding may yet emerge post-publication of *Business Planning for Games*. These are common enough to have been witnessed in industry across the globe; even then, it really boils down to the needs of the project and the paradigm of the founders that will inevitably lead to the choice of funding (if any). Remember things can go wrong and this needs to be considered when balancing the need for funding any aspect of the project and the longer-term aspirations for the founders.

8.2.1 11 Finance Methods to Consider

8.2.1.1 C Partners   These can be complicated and will always need some form of legal counsel to ensure things are structured in a fair manner for all parties involved. The 'C' stands for corporate, which may put some of the more alternative readers off. But think about it. If you have a big corporation on your side, one that is willing to adopt you and the project into their corporate structure, it will mean the project has a much more solid foundation from which to create the game(s) you want to create.

If this route to financing the project looks appealing, it might be worth seeking corporate partners that are on the periphery of the games sector and not game producers. The established studios will often have a paradigm that may exclude your genre of game. Convincing them to partner with you may be a bigger issue than you first thought. It is always worth looking beyond the immediate commercial organisations in the games sector you are seeking to get established in and try to think more widely.

An alternative is to seek a smaller but established game producer that might have an interest in exploring the possibilities you bring to their market. Be it a new game, a new take on an existing game, or the opportunity to explore new geographical areas with these games. Any of these scenarios might be of interest to both you and the corporate partner.

8.2.1.2 Contingency Marketing

- Is it possible to only pay an online influencer if they have a positive impact on profits?

There is obviously a need to build some relationship with the influencer and to ensure they are on point with both their own values and the values embedded in the project. But this could be a huge advantage if you are both aligned with the purpose of the project.

Another example would be a social or community building game where people are being brought together to be introduced to others in their local community. Let us imagine the theme of the game is around local produce, especially fruit and vegetables. Now imagine you find an influencer who is an advocate for producing locally grown fruit and vegetables. There is an obvious synergy where the two parties can benefit one another with the potential to have a far further reach than just a local concern or project. Or looking more broadly, consider other media forms. Could you get help from a local newspaper by offering a monthly column on games. They get content and you get content and you get some free space in local media.

8.2.1.3 Contract Retainer This takes some grit to pull off and there is often a need to underplay the reliance the project has on securing the retained finances. Imagine you have developed a serious game for a local council that is encouraging people to walk more as opposed to using their car. The Council agrees to the game being developed with the budgets you have all agreed. Now you can approach the Council and ask for some money upfront (say a fourth or a third of the value of the contract). This means you get some cash upfront to start work on the project.

This needs to be positioned to the client as something that will benefit them as well as yourself. They want the game produced on time and to the quality standards they expect, by retaining you they get some of these standards and more but, of course, they need to put some skin in the game. They need to 'retain' you and your focus on this game.

8.2.1.4 Crowdfunding One of the most refreshing ways to get funding and validation for your game is through crowdfunding. There are five models of crowdfunding that give us the acronym DREIM:

- Donation for social projects.
- Reward for projects that can offer an item in return for the money received – a form of shopping.
- Equity shares for projects that can offer shares in the company.
- Interest for projects that can raise debt from a crowd (many restrictions apply).
- Mixed for projects that want to utilise two models at contrasting times.

(Buckingham, 2015)

This author has been an advocate of crowdfunding for many years, crowdfunding remains one of the most intriguing forms of raising capital as it encapsulates not just the money but also education and engagement with the CUPs, with a strong focus on your game. This is an important aspect that often gets overlooked in business plans that want to utilise crowdfunding. It is not just about the money!

It can be used to validate the game. By putting it out there, you get to see how agents in the crowd react to your idea. You may even get some help to develop certain aspects of the game. These insights, provided by the agents in the crowd, can add greater value than you alone could have perceived. More than this, you can get the crowd to engage with you and take them along on the journey as the game gets developed.

8.2.1.5 Debt   Debt has changed in the last few years with the introduction of crowdfunding and the possibility of being able to raise debt from a group of strangers. Challenger banks in the UK, have also been established with varied degrees of success. The problem, as we touched on in Section 4.3, is that creative industries often fare worse at raising debt than comparable businesses. It is not always the institutional suppliers that are at fault either. As Fraser & Lomax (United Kingdom, 2011) highlighted, the issue can be that the creative industry project leader may not fully comprehend the levels of security the lender requires, and, so, deals sometimes do not materialise because the party seeking the debt backs away from the deal when they realise the levels of security being demanded against the debt being created. The perceived risks are simply too high or the security demands are perceived as unjust.

Added to this is the growing realisation that there is good and bad debt. Good debt is debt that leads to the project being able to economically sustain itself and turn the cost of the debt into profit. Bad debt on the other hand is characterised as a short-term fix that can add to the risks associated with the starting of a project and frequently act as a drain on the limited financial resources available. Good debt adds value, bad debt might get you out of a temporary fix, but it will drain financial resources over the longer term.

8.2.1.6 Equity In accounting terms, when we talk about equity in private firms, we mean the founders own money that has been used to get the project started. Let us say Rez starts her project with £5,000 of her own savings. Rez has started with £5,000 owner's equity.

Students have been confused with the term equity in the context of companies that sell shares; these are not private firms, and here the term equity refers to the value that these shareholders would receive if the company were bankrupt, all debts paid and then the shareholders divide the remaining residue cash.

8.2.1.7 Factoring This is a little opaque and it is fair to say that some in the business press have viewed factoring as a negative finance instrument because it can indicate a business is in distress. It works on the principle that a project generates invoices for the service it provides, which will be settled in a few months' time. In the meantime, these invoices can be used as security against borrowing cash. The reason factoring is sometimes considered a negative is that businesses that use factoring have been perceived as having mismanaged their cash flow and need quick injections of cash to pay bills.

There are many reasons for cash flow problems, it might be that the business in question (let us call it the Gamez Bizz) is chasing revenue and disregards the profit margin they make on this trade. This means that although Gamez Bizz may have many customers, all paying on time, the profit is small and not enough to make the trade worthwhile. A crucial point to be remembered is that customers are needed, but making a decent profit is essential for survival.

The way factoring works is quite straightforward. Gamez Bizz has an issue with their cash flow, so they decide to exchange their invoices for cash up front with a third party (like a bank). In effect they have sold their invoices, and this is how factoring is considered in the accounts – it is an exchange.

Gamez Bizz are going to have to pay for the convenience of having the cash up front, but this also means settlement of the invoice is no longer their concern, this now rests with the third party. That means they lose even more of the money that they would have received had they not had to enter a factoring deal for the cash. There is often a sense of urgency with factoring, and this is once again a reason it could be considered a sign of potential financial mismanagement.

8.2.1.8 Family, Friends, and Fools The most basic form of funding with the most stress, even when things go well. These are the groups of people in our lives that often want us to do well in life. They have a personal stake beyond the pecuniary, they have the peculiar!

This is a risk of extraordinary proportions because if things go wrong, if family and friends lose money, how will this affect the relationship you have with these people? There may be feelings of being obliged to help, even when there may be strong personal perceptions that suggest the project will fail. This can place a considerable strain on interpersonal relationships.

Also, consider the opposite, what if the project is a tremendous success. How will this impact these relationships? Will people feel isolated? Taken advantage of? Jealous? There are many aspects to consider before accepting funds from these people, even when the intentions are well meaning and offered as an attempt to be helpful.

8.2.1.9 Grants/Awards There are lots of different grants and awards available for both commercial and social businesses. In the creative industries, these can be especially competitive and can require a lot of work to complete the application processes. Anyone looking at grants or awards should also consider big corporations as they often have associated philanthropic units that administer these. Besides these, there are the more traditional routes to grants and awards like local government start-up schemes.

8.2.1.10 Make-on-Demand This is a bit of a cheat, as it is not a funding method per se. Stock is often an expensive use of finances. It can also be a severe drain on resources if you cannot subsequently distribute the units you had predicted. An alternative would be to produce on demand. This is a blatant steal from the book industry where print-on-demand has been in service to budding authors for several years now. But this is also possible within the games sector. It might mean some thorough research and a reduction in the profit margins for the games being produced, but it can also mean greater levels of control while market validation for the game is being sought.

8.2.1.11 Supplier Terms   This often results from a relationship being established with the supplier. Let us imagine that the supplier you use has terms and conditions that state that invoices need to be settled within 30 days. But because you have a good relationship with a supplier, they may extend the period to, say, 120 days. This provides you with more favourable terms and a longer period in which to settle the account. It provides you with some breathing space while also establishing a deeper sense of trust between you both. 120 days is not likely, and you need to show some respect for your suppliers, they are in the business of supplying you and have cash flows to consider.

However, there might also be some additional benefits for the supplier in terms of PR (Public Relations). If you are happy to talk about this supplier and the way they have helped you (without giving too much information away), then this could create a win-win situation. In PR terms, a good example would be the big supplier helping the little project get started and add value for some specific local group or the economy more widely. Either way, it is a positive impression being portrayed in the PR exercise.

8.3 Break-Even

Before we get into the break-even calculations and how this is going to affect a business plan, costs need explaining. The costs are divided between the things that do not change with the number of things produced and the costs that do change because of the number of things produced. These are termed *fixed* and *variable* costs as we encountered in Chapter 8.

Fixed and variable costs are important as these need to be calculated to provide you with the true point of break-even in the financial forecasts provided in the plan. Break-even is an essential calculation for the reader and the founding team of the project as this will determine at what point the project is neutral in terms of the expenditure and the revenues. In other words, it tells us when these things will be in balance. The sales being generated are greater than the costs of producing our game.

Break-even can be thought of as a milestone as it is rare for a project to lapse back into a situation where the sales do not allow for the costs of the project to be covered and indeed sales should be increasing from this point as a profit, with potential for growth, is made. Therefore, business plans will often include a nice summary on the break-even and a graphic demonstrating to the reader when the break-even point is predicted to be breached (see Figures 8.1 and 8.2).

There are several ways to calculate the break-even point for a project, but one rule always applies when making this calculation. The higher the fixed costs the more this is likely to push your break-even further into the future. The golden rule is to try and beg or borrow the fixed cost assets you need to get the project started. As an example, imagine a card deck needs to be printed with a specialist printer that trims the size and automatically sorts the cards into a specific order. The printer costs £10,000 to buy outright and then there are maintenance costs that work out to £2000 per month. That means that £12,400 will need to be spent on this asset in the first fiscal year. If sales are below this figure, then the project will be making a loss. Remember too, beside the printer, there will be other expenses for the project.

If, on the other hand, the project could rent the printer for the specific days it needed to produce the cards, the outright cost may be much lower. The cost per unit of deck of cards may be higher, meaning that the profit margin is reduced, but the outlay at the start is hugely reduced. This means the break-even can be shorter in time than would have been the case when the printer is purchased.

Renting is demonstrated in the example in Figure 8.1, while the second example in Figure 8.2 clearly shows a much higher revenue is needed to reach the break-even point.

In the first example, the revenues are increasing at a steady rate and the break-even is 160 units being sold with sales revenues being generated around the £13 mark. But as the variable costs are low, the point of break-even is also likely to be quick. The costs (fixed and variable added together) are initially much lower.

Compare this with the second example. In this scenario, we can see that the variable costs start much higher and the break-even is

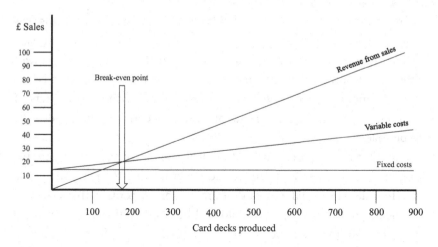

Figure 8.1 Break-even example 1.

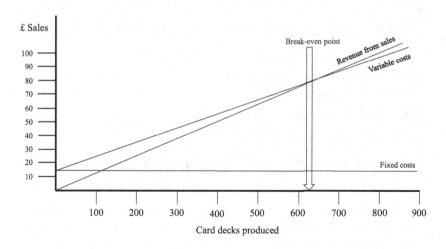

Figure 8.2 Break-even example 2.

around sales of £65 (about 610 units being sold). A stark difference. Now these are simple examples to demonstrate the point about the purchasing of assets. The hope is that it can demonstrate the need to take account of the things that are essential and the things that are nice to have, but not essential, in getting the project started.

The golden rule is always to seek a way to avoid paying for unnecessary resources that could be hired or otherwise utilised. But this comes with a caveat. The project in the first example (Figure 8.1) may soon need to purchase the equipment that the project in the second example bought at the start of their trading. It might be that this was a smarter move if the price of these assets is likely to increase significantly in the near future. Purchasing it at the start may also mean that the resource could be hired out to other projects when it is not in use, generating more cash for the project. As with most aspects of business planning, there are lots of things to consider and trade-offs to be made.

Another big issue, especially for early-stage projects, is the generation of sufficient profits to make the effort needed to create the game worthwhile. For social games that are not profit centric, this is less of a concern, but the warning should still be heeded. Finding customers is rarely a simple task and it can take considerable effort to convince these people to act and purchase from you. If you have stated five different segments of the market you are communicating with, then you need to be aware which ones will be the most profitable.

Let us imagine you have labelled the five segments as follows:

S1: are females aged 18–24.
S2: are non-binary aged 18–24.
S3: are males aged 25–34.
S4: are females aged 25–34.
S5:   are females aged 35–44.

Revenues generated from each segment breaks down as follows:

S1: 15%
S2: 15%
S3: 40%
S4: 20%
S5: 10%

So, you have your simple segments, and you know how much each segment generates in terms of revenue. Now you need to know how much profit each segment produces for the project (after *all* expenditures, i.e., net profit) from the revenues they generate. This breaks down as follows:

S1: 8%
S2: 7%
S3: 2%

S4: 3%
S5: 4%

We can see that S3 and S4 are low (5% compared with 19% for the other three segments combined). The question that should then be asked is this:

- If S3 and S4 were to be dropped, would the margins from S1, S2, and S5 increase because you would be able to focus on these segments more?

Put another way, if the effort needed to sell to S3 and S4 were redirected towards the other segments, would this result in an increase in profit for these three segments?

Dropping S3 and S4 will result in initial drop in revenue, 60% no less, this is huge. Equally, it may be that by chasing the revenue that S3 and S4 generate the project is missing an opportunity to work smarter and gain greater profit from a smaller customer base.

This is a far simpler example than you will face in the real world as you get out there and start trading. The intention is to demonstrate how this can affect the break-even and the differences in revenue and profit. There are many more variables that you will encounter in the real world. But by being aware of the differences between these aspects, the hope is you will be able to produce a better business plan with greater justifications for the choices you make.

8.4 Cash Flow

There is an old aphorism in business circles that turnover equals vanity, profit equals sanity but cash is still king. By cash of course, it means money in the bank. Cash flow in its most basic form is about the ebb and flow of money through the accounts of the project. There should be a diligent, almost obsessional, check on the cash situation in your accounts.

This is important as it means there is an understanding of the money owed to the project, the money the project owes to others, and the cash balance in the bank. Knowing these three things will help keep things balanced and prevent things from suddenly jolting from

Table 8.1   Monthly Sales Predictions

GAME	PRICE	MONTH 1	MONTH 2	MONTH 3	MONTH 4	MONTH 5	MONTH 6	SUB TOTAL
Decko	9.99	12	14	30	35	40	42	173
Mecko	11.99	20	75	70	75	85	100	425
Month totals		£359.68	£1039.11	£1139.00	£1248.90	£1418.75	£1618.58	£6824.02

having cash in the bank to not having cash in the bank and owing bills to suppliers that are due now, or worse still, overdue.

For the start-up game project, the initial cash flow will be a predicted one. There is no trading that has taken place. That means for the business plan this aspect must be based on the sales forecasting you have done, and the predictions made about the level of profit that can be generated from the revenues of this trading. Sales forecasting is an exercise that will lead to sound predictions about the number of units being distributed each month and the revenues this will generate. Table 8.1 is a simple forecast tool. The first column is the game that will be traded. There is the possibility for two games in this example, Decko and Mecko, but if you have less, delete the rows not needed and likewise if you have more games to offer add rows as necessary.

The price column is for the unit price per game. For example, if Decko retails for £9.99, enter £9.99 in the second column in the row for Decko. Then repeat for all games as in the example Table 8.1.

The monthly columns are where the total unit sales are entered. Each month is entered for each individual game. The column ends with the monthly totals in monetary terms. In our example, in Table 8.1, Decko distributed 30 games in month three, while Mecko distributed 70 games in the same month. The gross income can be worked out as follows:

Decko distributed 30 games @ £9.99 (30 x £9.99) = £299.70
Mecko distributed 70 games @ £11.99 (70 x £11.99) = £839.30

Therefore, the monthly total is £299.70 + £839.30 = £1139.00 (in month three).

Do this for all games for each month and this will provide you with the sales forecast for the year.

As with all references to the volume of trade you can predict, it is important that this is based on empirical insights and not figures that are guessed or even worse, plucked out of thin air. To be convincing in the business plan, they need to be based on some hard evidence about the market and the conditions of that market. Things can and do change, which the reader should understand. These are forecasts about the future that come without the possibility of hindsight. Even so, these figures need to be based on solid projections.

Having now worked out the predicted sales forecast, the attention can now turn to the forecasted cash flow statement. Again, this is in the form of a table. Whereas sales forecasts are quite simple in terms of the number of columns and rows, the cash flow provides the reader with much more depth. It is a representation of the ebb and flow of money in and out of the project as revenues are gained and expenditure realised.

The standard protocol for the cash flow is to first present the revenues (or income) for the business as a set of rows for each income label. For example, we will use the sales forecast for the games Decko and Mecko above and we can imagine this person also doing some consulting work for other companies.

There are diverse ways to present these incomes, but by using the double column and adding the monthly totals together at the bottom and then adding the rows together across the table, it acts as a double check for the figures – you know that the columns must be right as they arrive at the same figures as the rows. In Table 8.2, we can see that for the first six months of trading, the project made a healthy £8824.02, based on all the income-generating activities (sales of the game plus some consulting work).

Now comes the expenditure. Every project will have some unique things they will need to spend money on; for this reason, the entries in examples in Tables 8.2 and 8.3 are very generic in nature. Table 8.3 has some generic expenditures with a brief explanation.

The cash flow itself will look something like the example in Table 8.4.

Table 8.2 Cash Flow Income

INCOME	JANUARY	FEBRUARY	MARCH	APRIL	MAY	JUNE	**TOTAL**
Sales	£359.68	£1039.11	£1139.00	£1248.90	£1418.75	£1618.58	**£6824.02**
Consulting	£0	£200.00	£400.00	£0	£600.00	£800.00	**£2000.00**
Total	£359.68	£1239.11	£1539.00	£1248.90	£2018.75	£2418.58	**£8824.02**

Table 8.3   Cash Flow Expenditure Titles

EXPENDITURE	EXPLANATION
Ads/Market	Advertising and marketing, including business cards and flyers.
Banking	Bank charges.
Cap Items	Capital items, the equipment you need to trade.
Comms	Communications, including phone and internet connectivity.
*Drawings	The money you pay yourself as sole trader or partnership *only*.
Hosting	Website and other social media expenses.
HP	Hire purchase and leasing fees.
Insurances	All insurances related to the project.
Loan Costs	If a loan has been taken out, the interest paid is an expenditure.
Materials	The things you need to produce the game.
Other	What other expenses that do not fit elsewhere on this list?
Post	Postage is still entered as a separate entry in the cash flow.
Premises	Rent and rates you pay for the premises.
Pro fees	Professional fees for accountant or software you need.
Repairs	To the machines, or the building, you operate from.
Stationary	The stationary you need to operate well.
Stock	The stock you hold.
Tax	Taxes you must pay as a trading entity.
Transport	Transportation costs incurred for the project.
Utilities	Electricity, gas, and water.
Wage/NI/Pen	Wages, national insurance, and pensions paid for those employed by you.

Table 8.4   Example Cash Flow Expenditures

EXPENSE	JANUARY	FEBRUARY	MARCH	APRIL	MAY	JUNE	TOTAL
Ads/Market	£10	£10	£30	£30	£100	£100	£280
Banking	£0	£0	£0	£0	£180	£0	£180
Cap Items	£1000	£300	£0	£0	£0	£0	£1300.00
Comms	£15.00	£15.00	£15.00	£15.00	£15.00	£15.00	£90.00
*Drawings	£0	£50.00	£0	£0	£0	£0	£50.00
Hosting	£20.00	£20.00	£20.00	£20.00	£20.00	£20.00	£120.00
HP	£0	£0	£0	£0	£0	£0	£0
Insurances	£150.00	£0	£0	£0	£0	£0	£150.00
Loan Costs	£0	£0	£0	£0	£0	£0	£0
Materials	£150.00	£0	£80.00	£0	£0	£100.00	£330.00
Other	£25.00	£0	£0	£20.00	£30.00	£0	£75.00
Post	£5.00	£4.00	£2.00	£0	£0	£0	£11.00
Premises	£400.00	£400.00	£400.00	£400.00	£400.00	£400.00	£2400.00
Pro fees	£0	£400.00	£0	£0	£0	£0	£400.00
Repairs	£0	£0	£0	£0	£0	£0	£0

(*Contnined*)

Table 8.4 (Continued)   Example Cash Flow Expenditures

EXPENSE	JANUARY	FEBRUARY	MARCH	APRIL	MAY	JUNE	TOTAL
Stationary	£85.00	£0	£0	£10.00	£0	£0	£95.00
Stock	£0	£0	£0	£0	£0	£0	£0
**Tax	£0	£0	£0	£0	£0	£0	£0
Transport	£40.00	£15.00	£10.00	£0	£25.00	£75.00	£165.00
Utilities	£80.00	£75.00	£83.00	£89.00	£67.00	£55.00	£449.00
Wage/NI	£0	£0	£0	£0	£0	£0	£0
Total	£1980.00	£1289.00	£640.00	£584.00	£837.00	£765.00	**£6095.00**

A gross profit was made of £2729.02. This was worked out by taking the total income (£8824.02) and then subtracting the total expenditure (£6095.00). This example is for six months; it is there for demonstration purposes and the cash flow you will need for your business plan will need to cover 12 months. The headings may remain the same and the principles of presenting the income first followed by the expenditure is a standard that is time honoured and should be used in your business plan.

* Drawings. This needs some clarity as the rules are different for sole traders and partnerships versus limited company directors in the UK. As sole traders or partners the money taken for personal expenses is classified under the drawings heading, while for a limited company these are classified under the wages (or salary) heading.

** Tax will be added at the year end when we know the final trading figures (profit or loss). At this stage we are dealing with the first six months.

References

Buckingham, C. (2015), *Crowdfunding Intelligence*, London: LID.

United Kingdom (2011), *Department for Business Innovation and Skills, Access to Finance for Creative Industry Businesses*, London: Crown Copyright.

9

Introduction

Business Planning for Games now moves from the more traditional headings in level one to a more creative way to think about the business plan writing process. Level two is concerned with your own interpretation and thoughts about how you will tackle the sections of the plan you want to include. The headings in level two change as this is intended to be a more dynamic place for you to work through some of the ideas and visions you have for your project.

There are 12 headings in this level:

- Game
- Opportunity
- Goals
- Customers
- Success
- Strategy
- Marketing
- Partners
- Finance
- Resources
- Operations
- Model

Each of the 12 headings relate directly to the ones you encountered in level one. These are presented differently as this is the space for you to doodle and jot down thoughts about the areas covered in level one. But equally important is to help you navigate the context of the various headings for your business plan. No two plans will be identical, even when people are working on the same project. We all have our own views and our own biases to contend with, our own values, and our own perceptions about what is important to have in the plan.

 DOI: 10.1201/9781003352594-9

Level two, in many ways, is your opportunity to express these individualistic perceptions while allowing you to make the case for these ideas and ways of thinking. These may not have emerged had you simply just responded to the headings in level one.

For this reason, we suggest you be creative in your approach to the 12 worksheets in level two. Try doing this section in three rounds (or versions). The first using only images, the second adding some basic text to the images, and then a final version with the images removed but building on the remaining text so you have a more detailed overview. Doing this will take longer to complete, but it will also enlighten you to the process of writing and help create a stronger plan.

The aim of level two is to take away some of the anxiety you may feel when asked to produce a business plan, especially for people on the more creative spectrum. The idea of writing a business plan can be demotivating and present a barrier to getting creative with ideas and perceptions of our own abilities to produce something special, something that can be taken seriously by a market, and something that might be needed by someone out there in the real world.

We start with the clock face. The 12 headings for the worksheets that follow are mapped out in this second part of the book. These appear like the hours on a traditional clock face and can be used to help guide you as you work through the sections needed in your plan.

Start wherever you feel best for you, some people like to start with 'opportunity' while others may find their starting point is elsewhere. Again, this helps to emphasise the individual nature of this approach – there is no right or wrong way to complete the sheets that follow. However, they have been presented in a linear fashion in level two as this is an optimal approach for the purposes of this book.

Each heading will have a unique set of questions to consider. Some, like worksheets 03 (Goals) and 09 (Partners), will have just a few questions, while others have more. This is not an indication of importance or how long you should spend on these sheets but it merely means that the time spent on worksheets 03 and 09 will be more intense, with only a few questions to answer. It might also help to use the clock face of the headings below as a kind of checklist against the progress you are making. Feel free to print the page below and keep it somewhere visible with notes or doodles to help remind you of the progress you are making or things to consider doing next.

Each sheet has a row at the top with four sections:

- Project name is the name of the project this sheet refers to. It may be that you are working on more than one project at any time and so it will be less confusing to include the name of the project this sheet refers to.
- Date can either be the date the sheet gets worked on or the deadline for completion of this sheet. If you use the latter, be realistic about how long it will take to complete.
- Version is the version of the project or the sheet you are working on. As you work up the sheet and add more detail, it might be worth keeping track of the number of versions you have created. If you need to go back and look-up past ideas, this can be better facilitated if you know the version you need.
- Authors(s) are the people working on the sheet. If you are working in teams on these sheets, it can be beneficial to have allocated certain people to specific sheets and task them with completing that sheet. Having the names of the person or people responsible might save some headaches later.

10

WORKSHEET 01

Game

DOI: 10.1201/9781003352594-10

1 Game

Project name	Date	Version	Author(s)
1.1 Identify the games experience:		1.4 Emotional impact of this game:	
		1.5 Quantification of this impact:	
1.2 When does this game get played?		1.6 Nearest competition:	
1.3 Who will find this game useful?		1.7 Weaknesses in your competition:	

This worksheet supports your understanding of...

10.1 The Game Experience

This is a demanding thing to explore. It first requires you to put yourself in the shoes of the player or user. But of course, unless you have play-tested the game, then this is speculation. But even speculation can help you think about the experiences of the players or users. It is best to focus on the players at this stage rather than users. The user may be making use of the game in certain contexts, but that does not always mean they experience the playing of the game. Level One Section 1.2 can help with the focus of this box.

10.2 When Does This Game Get Played?

During the day at work, at night for fun, to kill time while waiting, or in a social setting after people have had drinks or a meal together. These times matter as they can impact the messages the game sends out in terms of marketing. Knowing the times and settings the game gets played creates a very distinct flavour for the game. This is unique and should be celebrated. Level One Section 1.1 can inspire this box.

10.3 Who Will Find This Game Useful?

This comes down to the jobs the CUPs do. If they are a single parent in need of some entertainment, this is quite different from a business manager seeking to train their people on aspects of the workflow they will encounter. The motivations are different, and this gets reflected in the utility of the game. It may also be true that there are multiple CUPs to consider. Embrace the differences and ensure you capture the essence of why they find utility in the game. Level One Sections 4.5 and 8.1 might inspire the content in this box.

10.4 Emotional Impact of This Game

How do you measure love, hate, warmth, or disgust? There are a wide variety of emotions CUPs may encounter. The first task then is to identify the most salient emotions they are likely to experience and then decide how to measure these, for example, happiness. To measure this, the playtests could ask CUPs to circle one of three faces on a questionnaire; one sad, one neutral, and one happy, depending on how they felt interacting with the game at various stages. It is a simple method that can provide some profound insights. Level One can be helpful in getting you to think about these aspects of the game and how to communicate these in the business plan.

10.5 Quantification of This Impact

Impact can be measured by looking at the outcomes of the CUP interaction with the game. For the manager in a company wanting to demonstrate the workflow to her colleagues (the players), it may be that the impact is educational, the players have learned the pattern of the workflow in the company. In another scenario, could the game provide a fun engaging time for families to play together? Quite different impacts but each important in their own way. Level One Sections 5.2 and 6.1 might help to add some context for you.

10.6 Nearest Competition

Now we move into the business areas of the games market. Who are these organisations and why are they thought of as competition? It may be that they do not develop games per se but are on the periphery of the market. For example, do they produce assets for games producers or provide copy writing services? It may be that these are competitors that need to be considered even though they are not game producers themselves (see Level One Section 4.5).

10.7 Weaknesses in Your Competition

Now we must start to think strategically about their offer and the things they do. Where are the weaknesses in the offer they make to the market? Why are these considered weaknesses? How does this knowledge help your project? These are vital questions and can be framed differently depending on the game and your own ability to comprehend what's important for the project here. Level One Section 2.1 might be helpful.

11

WORKSHEET 02

The Opportunity

DOI: 10.1201/9781003352594-11

2 Opportunity

Project name	Date	Version	Author(s)
2.1 Crucial success:		2.2 Risks:	
2.3 Clear values:		2.4 Game novelty:	
2.5 Market share:		2.6 Values & goals aligned:	

This worksheet supports your understanding of...

11.1 Crucial Success

As will be noted in Section 5.1, success can be in many forms. But what is crucial to the success of this game? It may be the quality of the suppliers or the timely delivery of the game for the customer. These do not have to be complex areas, but knowing what factors are crucial to the success of the game will enhance the potential of 'success' in a market.

11.2 Risks

What are the risks associated with the project? What form do these risks take, how can they be minimised, and how likely are they to happen? Knowing this will help the project look much more per-suasive for the reader of the business plan. It will provide the reader with the confidence needed to see this plan in a positive light. But of course, the risks need to be identified and assessed for their impact and the likelihood of affecting the project. Align these with Level One Section 4.4.

11.3 Clear Values

This brings the focus back to purpose. Can the values embedded in the game be clearly articulated and understood by the reader of the business plan? Can these be used to better position the game in the mind of the CUPs? Another aspect to consider is if this project is in balance with your personal ambitions (see Level One Section 2.2).

11.4 Game Novelty

How does this game stand out in a crowded market? What attracts CUPs to the game and more importantly influences their purchasing decision? These elements should be implicit as in worksheet 01 (The Game), in this box you are being asked to articulate this value in a more explicit way. Most games have elements that they build on with existing offers to the market, but your game is not going to be a direct copy of these games, there will be some added elements that can be bragged about in this box.

11.5 Market Share

How big is the market and realistically, based on the research done so far (Level One Chapter 5), what share of this market can you predict selling to? How sustainable is this share? Are the predictions for this market to grow? All essential areas to cover for the project, explaining these variables about the market that will help the business plan become more convincing for the reader.

11.6 Values and Goals Aligned

Values and the overall goals will need to be outlined, but do these contradict one another? If not, great, but even a small chink in the view of these can have devastating outcomes for the business plan. In this box, you can think about the values and the goals (see Sections 1.3 and 1.4 of Level One) and articulate how they work to reinforce the project and make the strategy stronger (see Section 3.1 of Level One).

12

WORKSHEET 03

Goals

DOI: 10.1201/9781003352594-12

3 Goals

Project name	Date	Version	Author(s)

3.1 Financial aspirations:

3.2 Quantification of generic aspirations:

3.3 Conflicts and compromises:

This worksheet supports your understanding of...

12.1 Financial Aspirations

These are important not just for the project, but also for the founders. What do you want to achieve in terms of financial goals in the production of the project? These need to be explained in ways that connect the values of the project with the values embedded in the culture that you wish to create to get things done. Level One Chapter 8 is an obvious place to find help for this box.

12.2 Quantification of Generic Aspirations

Beyond the finances, what do founders want to achieve with the project and how will this be measured? What milestones and benchmarks will be used to ensure these things are on target? Consider also the timing of these. When will these targets likely be met and what will be the next series of targets following this? Things to consider for inclusion in this box could be operational, strategic, or a social mission that needs tackling. This connects with Level One Chapters 2 and 3.

12.3 Conflicts and Compromises

Risks are covered in Worksheet 02 (Question 2.2). Here, we are asking if there are further areas of conflicts that emerge due to the scale and scope of the aspirations. This is an opportunity to identify these and outline how they are going to be mitigated against. These should be directly linked to the research outcomes identified in Level One Chapter 5.

13

WORKSHEET 04

Customers

DOI: 10.1201/9781003352594-13

4 Customers

Project name	Date	Version	Author(s)
4.1 Ideal customers:		4.2 Who pays?	
4.3 How much?		4.4 How often?	
4.5 At what point?		4.6 Research methodology and methods:	

This worksheet supports your understanding of…

13.1 Ideal Customers

Who are they and why are they ideal? What features do you look for in the customers that this project can satisfy? In this box, use the context of the personas created in Level One Section 1.2. But don't be afraid to create new personas here as this box allows you to sketch out more ideas of who has the potential to be included.

13.2 Who Pays?

Considering the CUPs, who makes the purchase? Is this the same person that the marketing is geared towards (see Level One Chapter 7)? If it's not, why not?

13.3 How Much?

What price point will be used and how do you know this is the optimal price point for the game? Research should be used here to back up the statements and facts being made about the game's price point (see Level One Chapter 5). Include the position of the brand (Level One Section 6.1) in this box as this will be critical in you being able to deliver a good match between the segments you want as CUPs (with emphasis on the customer) and the competition that is already established in this market.

13.4 How Often?

How frequently do they pay? This question is seeking to understand the patterns of the purchases that will happen. Seasons can be important in this question as could cycles of purchasing behaviour (Level One Chapters 5 and 8 could be relevant here).

13.5 At What Point?

Do they pay at the point of sale? Is there a subscription? Or do they get to play the game free for a period of time before having to pay?

It may also be a combination of these possibilities as more than one persona is identified as the customer. Attracting the various personas may require varied options to be available, each one optimal for a specific persona.

13.6 Research Methodology and Methods

What research have you done into the market and the game? What strategy (methodology) and tools (methods) have you used in the research you have conducted? To answer these questions, think about all the approaches you have used to get information (methodology) and the datasets used to gain useful information (methods). Level One Chapter 5 will be useful, as might Level One Section 8.1 on trade.

14

WORKSHEET 05

Success

DOI: 10.1201/9781003352594-14

5 Success

Project name	Date	Version	Author(s)
5.1 What is success?		5.2 How will it be quantified?	
5.3 Longer term plans:		5.4 Fail consequences:	

This worksheet supports your understanding of…

14.1 What is Success?

What will success look like to this project? There are many ways to measure success. Identifying what this means to the project is essential for the understanding of the market and the knowledge of how well a particular strategy is managing to meet the aims and the goals embedded in the purpose of the project (see Level One Chapters 2 and 3).

14.2 How Will It Be Quantified?

Putting numbers on success will mean the project can more easily be kept on track, especially when things are looking like they might not meet the deadlines or goals set. This may help with Worksheet 3 Question 3.2, as the generic things to be used as benchmarks and standards for the success of the project can be used as foundations for the quantification of the success factors in the project.

14.3 Longer-Term Plans

What are the longer-term plans for the project? Sell to the highest bidder? Keep it going for future generations? Answering these questions will add clarity for all stakeholders of the business plan. Having a clearly defined longer-term goal can also aid thinking on the way in which the culture of the project may change as things get scaled and growth is experienced. See Level One Section 1.1 for ideas on this element.

14.4 Fail Consequences

If things fail, what will be the fallout from this failure? Who gets affected and by how much? Some people will be impacted more than others and knowing how this might look can help the founder prepare for a future where the project is no longer viable. This should be considered in the context of risk from Level One Section 4.4.

15

WORKSHEET 06

Strategy

DOI: 10.1201/9781003352594-15

6 Strategy

Project name	Date	Version	Author(s)

6.1 STEEPLE analysis:

6.2 SWOT analysis:

6.3 Plan 'A':

6.4 Plan 'B':

This worksheet supports your understanding of...

15.1 STEEPLE Analysis

Conducting a STEEPLE is essential to help you answer the SWOT that follows. The most effective way to fill this box is to reiterate the seven STEEPLE questions over time. It is also more effective to be as straightforward as possible when providing answers. The more complicated you make this, the less likely it is that the reader will be able to follow the impacts you are predicting (if any of course). See Level One Chapter 5 for help.

15.2 SWOT Analysis

Remember to think about internal (strengths and weaknesses) and external (opportunities and threats) as you compile the SWOT analysis. Base the input in this box on the things that you considered in the STEEPLE analysis form above.

15.3 Plan 'A'

What is the best-case strategy for the project? Success will mean plan 'A' being realised, but how does this look and what shape does this take? Think about the success factors and the way this can be realised in the markets you want to enter.

15.4 Plan 'B'

If plan 'A' fails to meet the goals set, what will happen if the project is not a complete failure? What can be done with the remaining elements of the project? Could there be a plan B to help the project pivot and do something of value in another market?

16

WORKSHEET 07

Marketing

DOI: 10.1201/9781003352594-16

7 Marketing

Project name	Date	Version	Author(s)
7.1 Budgets:		7.2 How much?	
7.3 How often?		7.4 Where?	
7.5 Measurement:		7.6 Marketing objectives:	

This worksheet supports your understanding of...

16.1 Budgets

What budgets will be used to control the marketing for the project? Will there be different breakdowns for each element of the marketing strategy or will the budgets be allocated on more general terms? See Level One Section 8.1.

16.2 How Much?

How much do you have to spend on the variables that make-up the marketing of the game? Are these being allocated to optimise the overall strategy? How do you know? See Level One Chapter 7.

16.3 How Often?

This concerns the marketing activities and how frequently you communicate the value proposition to the audience. Level One Chapter 7 will help in this box, but also align this with Level One Chapter 6.

16.4 Where?

What channels will be optimal for this communication? Do not discount old-school media; print, radio, and TV are still options, if budgets allow.

16.5 Measurement

How are you to measure the impact of these various activities that go into the marketing of the game?

16.6 Marketing Objectives

In the first place, think about what you are marketing (see Level One Section 1.3). It may sound a bit obvious to you as the author, but for the reader of the business plan, it is not always clear why particular strategies and channels are being used. By taking the time to articulate them here, you can overcome any lack of understanding.

17

WORKSHEET 08

Resources

DOI: 10.1201/9781003352594-17

8 Resources

Project name	Date	Version	Author(s)
8.1 Needs are identified:		8.2 Chronology of needs present:	
8.3 Suppliers are identified:			

This worksheet supports your understanding of...

17.1 Needs Are Identified

What do you need from your partners to make this game a reality? Are there needs able to be fulfilled within a time frame and to a quality that helps you deliver to the market a product that meets the standards you want to deliver? Likewise, it might also help you think about how you nurture these relationships. See Level One Section 4.3.

17.2 Chronology of Needs

What is the most likely sequence of things needed to be satisfied before the next round of requirements are to be met? This can be easy to overlook but by taking the time to consider these elements, you can make a stronger case for the business plan and help add clarity for a reader that may otherwise have had perceptions of waste. It also offers you the opportunity to reflect on the needs for the game development and the timeline to assess, locate, negotiate, and take delivery of these things.

17.3 Suppliers Are Identified

Suppliers are the organisations or people that deliver on short-term contracts to a set standard. The sourcing of these may be through a bid process where different suppliers are requested to set out their quality, time to deliver, and price (among other things). By identifying who and where they are based, you can start to build a picture of potential suppliers. Once this is done, the focus then shifts to quality. Can they supply the quality you need to satisfy your standards? Add as much detail as you can about who are possible candidates to be suppliers.

18

WORKSHEET 09

Partners

DOI: 10.1201/9781003352594-18

9 Partners

Project name	Date	Version	Author(s)

9.1 Who and where?

9.2 Alternatives:

This worksheet supports your understanding of...

18.1 Who and Where?

These may overlap with the suppliers in Worksheet 08. In which case, you can spend less time on these profiles. Partners tend to be more flexible in the working relationships you have with them. They are often characterised as having longer-term relationships with the project. Some of these partners are non-game partners. They may work on the periphery of the games sector; therefore, you must state what they offer, for example, accountants, HR consultants, or social media partners. This box is probing for what they supply and the role they play in the development of the game. It might also help to state how long you will be (or have been) working with these partners.

18.2 Alternatives

Who else could do the job to offer the value you seek? This is important because if things go wrong with the partners, you are building relationships with, having a plan 'B' can save a lot of time and headaches. This is also worth noting that alternatives may be suppliers at present. Partners and suppliers are polars with the possibility of one poll morphing into the other and vice versa.

19

WORKSHEET 10

Finance

DOI: 10.1201/9781003352594-19

10 Finance

Project name	Date	Version	Author(s)
10.1 Seasons accounted for:		10.2 Sustainable revenue stream(s) set out:	
10.3 Cash flow, present & correct:		10.4 Logical record keeping strategy outlined:	

This worksheet supports your understanding of...

19.1 Accounting for Seasons

Virtually every project on the planet is affected by seasons. This is the change and shift in the patterns of CUP behaviour over the course of a period of time, most likely a 12-month period. In this box, you need to firstly explain what the season means for your project and then how they impact the cash flow projected for the project.

19.2 Sustainable Revenue Stream(s) Set Out

These need to be convincingly researched and detailed to show accuracy in the projections and to communicate with the reader of the plan how these will be generated, and the frequency of the volumes predicted (Level One Section 5.3 on Market Size might be helpful here).

19.3 Cash Flow

There should be three cash flows produced for internal use, these are: optimistic, practical, and pessimistic. In the external version, the optimistic or practical cash flows are shown for obvious reasons. Scenario planning in this way will help you make sense of the realities of trading once you start and help with strategic planning for the next few years. Each cash flow must be backed up with robust research and not just put together with figures plucked out of thin air.

19.4 Logical Record

What system will be used to keep track on the ebb and flow of money in/money out? This may seem a little odd, but by being meticulous about these smaller details the reader can be better persuaded that the project is authentic about taking responsibility for the operations of the project. It also may mean a cost associated with the recording keeping you choose (an online supplier for example), see Level One Section 4.5 for ideas.

20

WORKSHEET 11

Operations

DOI: 10.1201/9781003352594-20

11 Operations

Project name	Date	Version	Author(s)
11.1 Resources and partners linked:		11.2 Delivery channels identified:	
11.3 Methods of payment provided:		11.4 Terms of business present:	
11.5 Clear logical process explained:			

This worksheet supports your understanding of…

20.1 Resources and Partners Linked

Is there a clear link between the people the project wants to work with and the value they add to the project? There are many crossovers with Worksheets 08 and 09. Whereas in the above worksheets, you have merely outlined their existence, in this box you provide yourself with more detail and drill down on the links between these parties and the things they offer. When you sketch out these links make it clear for yourself why these are the best partners to deliver on these resources. Often, this is not just about the price, for example, working closely with a particular partner might help reduce your costs while also helping you develop a critical competitive advantage.

20.2 Delivery Channels Identified

How will the game be distributed and what kind of contracts does this involve? Addressing this question will be focusing on the partners (or suppliers) identified, but whichever channels are used, there will be costs associated with them. This box should be a more granular view of these channels and their associated costs.

20.3 Methods of Payment

How will payment be processed and what costs are involved with this process? Do these need any negotiations to be agreed on with third parties? For example, you may have agreed a price for a product to a particular customer, but maybe they want to use a method of payment that will have higher costs for your project. In this instance, could there be an alternative method that may reduce this cost?

20.4 Terms of Business

How long will people have to pay you? Does this need negotiating with CUPs? Is this clearly stated on the invoices you send out? If your project is offering different products to different customers, then this box needs to outline what the terms will be for each of these. It might be worth stating if any negotiations are needed or have taken place in this box.

20.5 Clear Logical Process Explained

This is not about the process of manufacturing or delivering the product but the process from the customer's perspective. From the first point of contact right through to the playing of the game, each step of the process needs to be articulated and explained. Note this box is oblong in shape. Could it be best to use a timeline in this box to explain the customer's journey? Is it also worth creating more of these timelines for each of the CUPs?

21

WORKSHEET 12

Model

DOI: 10.1201/9781003352594-21

12 Model

Project name	Date	Version	Author(s)

12.1 Model aligned with the vision & the aims:	12.2 Credible model for the opportunity:

12.3 Are alternatives considered?	12.4 Explicit reasoning provided:

This worksheet supports your understanding of...

21.1 Model Aligned with the Vision and the Aims

Does the model help to meet the vision and the goals of the project? Models can be adjusted to meet your demands, but they must also be logical and cohesive for the reader to understand in the context of the game being brought to market. Is there a competitive advantage to the model?

21.2 Credible Model for the Opportunity

Given the opportunity that you have identified, are the model and strategy thoughts optimal for the project's survival, aligned? If you are struggling with this question, continue this sentence: *The model makes sense for the project because...*

21.3 Are Alternatives Considered?

What alternative models have been considered? Why have these been discounted? It may be possible or even necessary to pivot in the future in which case these models can be re-examined. But right now, this box is asking you to justify where the weaknesses are in the other models.

21.4 Explicit Reasoning Provided

The whole thing needs to be cohesive and coherent for the reader. What checks have been made to ensure this is the case? Have you looked at the language you use and how you have positioned yourself against competition in the market?

Index

Pages in **bold** refer tables.

Printed in the United States
by Baker & Taylor Publisher Services